D0202799

Bill —

Thank you for your support. Best Wishes.

Jerry Gale

4/18/91

CONVERSATION ANALYSIS OF THERAPEUTIC DISCOURSE:
The Pursuit of a Therapeutic Agenda

Jerry Edward Gale

Volume XLI in the Series
ADVANCES IN DISCOURSE PROCESSES
Roy O. Freedle, Editor

ABLEX PUBLISHING CORPORATION
NORWOOD, NEW JERSEY

Copyright © 1991 by Ablex Publishing Corporation

All rights reserved. No part of this publication may be reproduced, stored in a retrieval system, or transmitted, in any form or by any means, electronic, mechanical, photocopying, microfilming, recording, or otherwise, without permission of the publisher.

Printed in the United States of America.

Library of Congress Cataloging-in-Publication Data

Gale, Jerry Edward.
    Conversational analysis of therapeutic discourse / by Jerry Edward
Gale.
       p. cm. — (Advances in discourse processes ; v. 41)
    Includes bibliographical references and index.
    ISBN 0–89391–705–2 (cl)
    1. Psychotherapy patients—Language. 2. Family psychotherapy.
I. Title. II. Series.
    [DNLM: 1. Communication. 2. Family Therapy—methods. 3. Outcome
and Process Assessment (Health Care) 4. Professional-Patient
Relations. WM 430.5.F2 G151c]
RC488.5.G35 1990
616.89′14—dc20
DNLM/DLC
for Library of Congress   90-14423
                                                  CIP

Ablex Publishing Corporation
355 Chestnut Street
Norwood, New Jersey 07648

Table of Contents

Preface to the Series

Roy O. Freedle
Series Editor

This series of volumes provides a forum for the cross-fertilization of ideas from a diverse number of disciplines, all of which share a common interest in discourse—be it prose comprehension and recall, dialogue analysis, text grammar construction, computer simulation of natural language, cross-cultural comparisons of communicative competence or other related topics. The problems posed by multisentence contexts and the methods required to investigate them, while not always unique to discourse, are still sufficiently distinct as to benefit from the organized model of scientific interaction made possible by this series.

Scholars working in the discourse area from the perspective of sociolinguistics, psycholinguistics, ethnomethodology and the sociology of language, educational psychology (e.g., teacher-student interaction), the philosophy of language, computational linguistics, and related subareas are invited to submit manuscripts of monograph or book length to the series editor. Edited collections of original papers resulting from conferences will also be considered.

Foreword

What can one learn from studying one session of psychotherapy? I think I'll let one of my teachers, the iconoclastic and uncommon therapist/psychiatrist Milton Erickson, answer.

> A professor of internal medicine, after reading a psychiatric report on a single instance of an untried medication administered to only one patient with lethal results proved much more than could possibly be desired. The nature and character of a single finding can often be more informative and valuable than a voluminous aggregate of data whose meanings is dependent on statistical analysis . . . Rather than proof of specific ideas, an illustration or portrayal of possibilities is often the proper goal of experimental work. (Erickson, 1953)

I've been telling my friends lately that I know I've made it into the world of fame and fortune (well, at least fame). My evidence is that someone has done a book on one of my therapy sessions. They look suitably impressed and a bit shocked. "How could somebody write a whole book on one session?," they ask. *Why* would anyone bother? This book is the answer to that question.

I was originally approached by Jerry Gale and asked if I had a session that I thought was representative of my work that he could use for some research towards his dissertation. I rather flippantly agreed and proceeded to forget about the matter. Several months later, however, Jerry followed up with a request for a videotape or audiotape of a session which I considered both representative and relatively successful. This was a difficult task. The therapy I do is predicated on the idea that each person is an exception and no session is typical. After some struggle, I decided on the session that is the subject of this book.

I was in for a surprise when Jerry sent me the preliminary draft of the dissertation he was writing. My work was not merely part of his dissertation research, it was the sole source of the analysis he was to do. I was flattered and interested to find what he would write about my work.

I have an elaborate explanatory model I use to describe my work, which I know has only a marginal relationship to what I actually do in therapy. Here was an opportunity to see my work through someone else's eyes and models and to learn something new about it.

I learned two major things from reading Dr. Gale's analysis that I hadn't realized before. One is that I talk for clients. Someone once said in preface to a question they asked during a workshop I was teaching, "I know you don't want to put words in your clients' mouths, . . ." I interrupted him to tell him that I did indeed want to put words in my clients' mouths and thoughts in my clients heads. Until I read Dr. Gale's analysis, I did not realize that I did this by "talking for" or being an alter ego for my clients.

The other realization was how much I talk over my clients' talk and ignore potentially unhelpful things that they say and then attribute agreement to them. Having read that, I have shared the realization with some of my clients, who have laughed and recognized the truth of the analysis. The funny thing about this is that the clients told me they hadn't realized I did this until I told them. After I told them, of course, they noticed it quite a bit.

And I guess that's the value of books like this. They get us to realize things we don't usually. To see things from new angles. And that is similar to what we try to do when we're doing good therapy: Get people to see things from new angles.

So, I can say thank you to Dr. Gale for his contribution to the work that I do. I hope those readers from psychotherapy-land, conversation analysis-land and ethnomethodology-land will find new territory similarly illuminated for them by Dr. Gales' map.

REFERENCES

Erickson, M. H. (1953, October) The therapy of a psychosomatic headache." *Journal of Clinical and Experimental Hypnosis, 4,* October: 2–6.

William Hudson O'Hanlon, M.S.
January 1990
Omaha, Nebraska

Preface

Language and conversation has long fascinated me with its magic. Early in my life as a young child, I had a speech impediment that taught me the importance of interactional properties of conversation. Growing older, I struggled with trying to understand how thoughts formed and how words emerged. While I was unable to find answers to those problems, I did pursue a career as a family therapist. As a therapist, I used the spoken word to help others improve their lives. When I discovered the world of Ericksonian hypnosis I became even more enchanted with exploring conversations and constructively using words to help my clients. While as a clinician I used my own experiences and training to improve my clinical skills, I was not satisfied with research methodologies (that I was familiar with at the time) that scientifically explored the clinical conversation.

As a doctoral student at Texas Tech University, while working on a project examining doctor-patient discourse, I got involved with ideas and people from the Department of Speech Communication. The world of ethnomethodology and conversation analysis were introduced to me at this time. I had found a method capable of transporting me down the road of examining the therapeutic process.

Embarking on this qualitative, discovery-oriented voyage, I wanted to explore and describe how language was used to elicit change, such that the participants could experience new meanings or actions in a clinical session. In order to critically examine any therapeutic conversation, it is important to appreciate the context in which the conversation evolved. Words are embedded within a variety of contexts and can have a variety of meanings dependent on those contexts. Conversation analysis was chosen as a methodology that could critically explore a therapeutic conversation while being sensitive to the various contexts.

However, in the same manner that meanings of words are embedded within frames of contexts, each reader/listener who participates in observing a dialogue (such as reading this book), also adds a new level of context with a new gloss of meaning. Therefore, each reader of this book brings her or his own world view/epistemology that will organize how she or he makes sense of what is written.

Indeed, this is one of the key points of the book, that participants of a conversation continuously create their own meaning, and demonstrate this meaning through their actions. Regardless of the degree of detail presented (Appendix B presents the entire session transcript) and the complexity of explanation provided, the reader will still make sense of the book from her or his own perspective. You, the reader, cannot see from my eyes or hear from my ears.

Conducting this study, I immersed myself in the data, and employed the constant comparative method of analysis (Glaser & Strauss, 1967). I listened and observed the 45 minute therapy session for approximately 80 hours. Throughout this process, the transcripts were continuously revised and improved. In the course of doing this analysis (nine months), many categories and descriptions were considered. As these categories emerged, there were several fellow researchers/mentors who were invaluable in helping me to define and articulate these descriptions. In particular, G. H. "Bud" Morris and Neal Newfield were extremely helpful in watching/listening to the session and discussing with me the details of the transcript and the categories emerging. Additionally, while at the 1989 International Communication Association conference, Anita Pomerantz was immensely helpful in offering suggestions and encouragement.

I do want to point out to the reader though, that in reading this study, it may appear as if the categories described in the book (as well as the husband's, wife's and therapist's agendas presented in Chapter 4) exist as ontological facts. Even the term "discovery-oriented research" implies that there is some "thing" out there to be found. For the purpose of this study, the notion of "discovery" entails that I began my analysis without *a priori* notions of what to expect. The categories and descriptions that emerged from immersing myself in observing and transcribing the session are descriptions that I found meaningful, useful and fitting to the data.

Therefore, it would be in error to read these descriptions as if they represent the "true" motives of the participants, or what the participants "really" thought. I did not know what these people were thinking. Rather, these categories and agendas are merely my descriptions of what I perceived as meaningful. This does not minimize the descriptions and conclusions presented in the analysis, but it does urge you, the reader, to consider carefully the meanings, understandings and conclusions you draw.

REFERENCES

Glaser, B. G. & Strauss, A. L. (1967). *The discovery of grounded theory: Strategies for qualitative research*. Chicago: Aldine Publishing Corporation.

ACKNOWLEDGEMENTS

These acknowledgements are to those people and ideas that have contributed to my researcher's lenses as well as to the merit of this book (as I take full responsibility for any demerits).

During the past two years many have been helpful in bringing forth this book. First, I could not have completed this project without the support of my loving wife, Barbara, who frequently shared me with my Kaypro and Norelco. I also deeply appreciate Bill O'Hanlon for his willingness to share his work with me to examine and "take apart." In the same manner, I owe my gratitude to the husband and wife of the therapy session, who agreed to allow the publication of the analysis of their session (and who, two years later are together and doing well).

I thank my dissertation committee, at Texas Tech University, of Neal Newfield, Bud Morris, Ray and Dorothy Becvar and Nancy Bell for their support, ideas, encouragement and efforts. Deepest appreciation goes to my friends Ron Chenail and Douglas Flemons who helped me to develop my ideas and directions. Thanks goes to Brad Keeney for opening up many possibilities of looking at the world. Thanks also to Shelly Green, Ann Nobel, Paul Douthit, my parents, Al and Lorraine Gale (who continuously believed in me), my father-in-law, Jerry Goren (who also believed in me), Robert Hopper (who demonstrated to me the importance of meditating with a stenographic foot pedal), Cloe and Max (who were always there), and the faculty and students at The University of Georgia who welcomed me to their program and encouraged me to complete this project. Thanks also go to Bill Mathews for first suggesting I talk to O'Hanlon. Also thanks to those fine people at Ablex Publishing Corporation, Roy O. Freedle, Barbara Bernstein, and Carol Davidson who supported my ideas, and helped in improving this book. Finally, thanks to so many others who were there with me in Lubbock Texas and Athens Georgia to dialogue with and help me clarify my thinking.

Chapter 1
Introduction

It is generally accepted that client changes are facilitated by the therapist's talk. How this change comes about, however, is still unclear. Szasz (1978) stated that

> seeing therapy as a conversation rather than cure thus requires that we not only consider the error of classifying it as a medical intervention, but we must look anew at the subject of rhetoric and assess its relevance to mental healing. (p. 11)

The research of this subject, though, is still in an early stage of development (Gurman, Kniskern, & Pinsof, 1986; Greenberg & Pinsof, 1986; Pinsof, 1988; Reiss, 1988; Wynne, 1988a).

The purpose of this study is to microanalyze the actual talk of a therapy case. Analyses of whole sessions (let alone an entire case) have seldom been done in the family therapy field (Haley & Hoffman, 1967; Keeney, 1986). The therapy office is a unique context in which the institution of psychotherapy (therapist and client interactions) is constructed and maintained.

Since the time when Anna O. labeled her therapy with Breuer (chronicled by Freud) as a form of "talking cure" (Russell, 1987), psychotherapy has expanded and improved on its repertoire of linguistic devices to affect therapeutic change for the clients. However, it was not until the late 1930s, with the advent of phonographic recordings that the actual talk of the therapist and client could be examined. The first person to take advantage of these recordings to investigate the properties of language was Carl Rogers (Rogers, 1942; Russell, 1987; Small & Manthei, 1986). Rogers (1942) hoped that with this new technology for recording the sessions, "psychotherapy [could] become a process based on known and tested principles, with tested techniques for implementing these principles" (p. 434).

Unfortunately, since that time, "those 'known and tested principles' have been extremely elusive" (Russell, 1987, p. 2). Small and Manthei (1986) suggest that possible reasons for these deficiencies include: (a) a "difficulty of establishing agreement on how to describe therapy in general terms in the face of the . . . . various specific theories" (p. 395), (b) the tendency to focus only on the client's talk and not the therapist's talk, and (c) the lack of researchers willing to do process research.

PROCESS RESEARCH

As recently as the late 1970s, process research was still in its infancy. The need for further development was apparent. Gurman and Kniskern (1978) reported that without developing a fundamental understanding of the very process of change, research in the family therapy field would be weak. Orlinsky and Howard (1978) stated that "it is essential to provide detailed specifications and observations of the actual process" (p. 310) in order to understand how psychotherapy change occurs. Process research has developed a great deal in the past decade. During this time, process research has moved "out of its infancy into toddlerhood" (Greenberg & Pinsof, 1986, p. 3).

Pinsof (1981) noted that "process researchers in particular have been individually oriented and have ignored, until very recently, family therapy as both a treatment modality and theoretical orientation" (p. 701). Gurman, Kniskern, and Pinsof (1986) report that in developing process research (as well as outcome research) of marital and family therapy, new conceptual understandings are needed. The cybernetic epistemology of family therapy "creates a new interpersonal gestalt that is not adequately addressed by the methods, procedures, and designs of individual therapy process research" (Gurman et al., 1986, p. 597). Therefore, as these authors point out, methodology and forms of analysis of process research are still being developed.

ETHNOMETHODOLOGY AND CONVERSATION ANALYSIS

It is the intent of the present study to help in this developing stage of process research by introducing a methodology that is new to the family therapy field, yet is particularly suited to family therapy. This method is the ethnomethodological and conversation analytic perspective, and it has just recently been applied to a family therapy setting (Buttny, 1990; Buttny & Lannamann, 1987). This methodology provides an approach toward analyzing contextual patterns that is consistent with a systemic and cybernetic epistemology. This sensitive, microanalytical approach, which has been used in sociology and speech communication for the past 20 years (Garfinkel, 1967; Heritage, 1984; Levinson, 1983; Schwartz & Jacobs, 1979), seeks "to discover the interpretive practices through which interactants produce, recognize, and interpret their own and others' actions" (Pomerantz, 1988, p. 361).

This study will employ conversation analysis to examine a one-session consultation/demonstration case of therapist William O'Hanlon. The case is ideal for this type of analysis because: (a) O'Hanlon's clinical work is theoretically defined, (b) it is a one-session consultation in which the entire context of the case is encapsulated in the transcripts of the session, (c) the case is seen as a successful case by both the therapist and the clients (O'Hanlon, personal communication, 1989; clients, personal communication, February 1990), and (d) the case was videotaped and audiotaped.

William O'Hanlon, outstanding presenter at the 1985 national convention of the American Association for Marriage and Family Therapy, is a well-respected clinician and author of family therapy and Ericksonian therapy books (O'Hanlon & Wilk, 1987; O'Hanlon, 1987; O'Hanlon & Weiner-Davis, 1989) and papers (1989). He is currently involved with a new approach in family therapy called solutions-orientated therapy (de Shazer, 1982, 1985; O'Hanlon, 1989; O'Hanlon & Wilk, 1987; O'Hanlon & Weiner-Davis, 1989).

John Weakland (1987), in the preface of O'Hanlon and Wilk's book, stated the need for the "transcripts of a complete session or a whole case" (p. viii) of O'Hanlon's clinical work. This study will provide such a transcript as well as a detailed analysis of how the interactive talk of the session is patterned. Conversation analysis will also be explored as a new methodology for family therapy research. This type of detailed, discovery-oriented research will: (a) provide a methodology sufficiently sensitive to discern patterns consistent with a systemic epistemology (Gurman et al. 1986; Pinsof, 1988; Schwartzman, 1984), (b) discover patterns of the institutional talk of family therapy, similar to the principles sought by Rogers (1942), and (c) offer clinicians new ideas and skills toward the advancement of family therapy as a new paradigm.

The ethnomethodological approach of conversation analysis introduces some unique features to the current process research of family therapy. Heritage (1984) points out that Garfinkel's approach toward understanding language "is not to be regarded as a matter of 'cracking a code' which contains a set of pre-established descriptive terms" which combine to yield meanings about the world (p. 139). Instead, "understanding language" is a matter of "understanding actions—utterances—which are constructively interpreted in relation to their contexts" (p. 139).

The distinction between traditional process research and conversation analysis is significant. Conversation analysis has no fixed agenda. Unlike traditional process research, conversation analysis is not searching for underlying entities or attitudes "which generate talk and behavior" (Potter & Wetherell, 1987, p. 55), but rather, it is a detailed examination of how the talk itself is a performative action that helps to both interpret and produce behaviors.

Conversation analysis is structured around variability rather than commonalities. With conversation analysis, context is seen as endogenous, as "generated within the talk of participants and, indeed, as something created in and through that talk" (Heritage, 1984, p. 283). This view of an endogenous context necessitates the detailed analysis of the conversation itself rather than the examination of verbal chunks removed from their natural context.

Heritage (1984) states that communication acts are doubly contextual in that each speech utterance is both context-shaped and context-renewing. Crediting Garfinkel (1967) for this notion, Heritage (1984) states:

> Each action is context-shaped in the ways in which it is designed and understood by reference to the environment of actions in which it participates. And it is context-renewing in the way that each action, in forming a new context to which the next will respond, will inevitably contribute to the environing sequence of actions within which the next be formed and understood. (p. 280)

The implication of this notion is that any institutional context, for example, jury deliberation room, physician's examination room, a crisis hotline, or a therapist's office can be researched through the talk that goes on in these settings. "It is within these local sequences of talk, and only there, that these institutions are ultimately and accountably talked into being" (Heritage, 1984, p. 290). As Garfinkel (1967) stated, "any setting organizes its activities to make its properties as an organized environment of practical activities detectable, countable, recordable, tell-a-story-aboutable, analysable—in short, accountable" (p. 33).

The above-mentioned assumptions of conversation analysis match well with a systemic, cybernetic epistemology. Conversation analysis eschews searching for causes, but rather, is an empirical approach that seeks to describe *how* human behavior works in a reflexive and interactive manner (Pomerantz & Atkinson, 1984). It is precisely because of reasons such as these that conversation analysis has much to offer to family therapy process research.

THE ORGANIZATION OF THE STUDY

Chapter 2 presents a review of the literature on process research from the perspective of both the individual therapy paradigm and the family therapy paradigm. Gaps in current family therapy process research is pointed out and an overview of conversation analysis is offered as a methodology to fill some of those gaps. Chapter 3 operationalizes the use of conversation analysis as a means for analyzing the marital session conducted by O'Hanlon.

Chapter 4 presents the results of the analysis of the transcripts and compares the patterns discerned with O'Hanlon's explanation of his epistemology. Chapter 5 discusses the results of the conversation analysis and their implications for understanding the therapeutic work of William O'Hanlon in particular and family therapy in general. Recommendations and conclusions for family therapy are discussed. The transcript of the entire session are included in Appendix B.

Safran, Greenberg, and Rice (1988) state that the researcher's use of clinical transcripts "is a conceptually demanding, methodological rigorous, and labor-intensive process which should not be relegated to the status of 'pilot work' which takes place before the 'real research' begins" (p. 15). This study is an example of such a process.

Chapter 2
A Review of Relevant Literature

In reviewing the individual psychotherapy and family therapy process research literature, an interesting commonality can be discerned. While leaders in the family therapy field (Auerswald, 1988; Bateson, 1972; de Shazer, 1982; Gurman & Kniskern, 1981; Gurman, Kniskern, & Pinsof, 1986; Hoffman, 1981; Keeney, 1982, 1983; Schwartzman, 1984; Stanton, 1988; Steier, 1985, 1988; Tomm, 1983; Wynne, 1988a, 1988c) have typically defined family therapy as a paradigm unique and distinct from the individual psychotherapy paradigm, these two "paradigms" share a common research heritage. This chapter presents literature reflecting the common heritage of these two paradigms as well as a review of ethnomethodology and conversation analysis. First, the methodologies of individual psychotherapy and family therapy process research, which share an emphasis on "exploratory, discovery-oriented research" aimed at the "change process" (Greenberg, 1989, p. 207), are examined. This perspective will be provided in order to build a framework for viewing the strengths and weaknesses of family therapy process research.

Secondly, an overview of ethnomethodology and conversation analysis is presented. It is argued that there are gaps in current family therapy process research methodologies that do not address certain features of systemic family therapy. The ethnomethodology of conversation analysis is presented as a methodology that can help fill these gaps.

PROCESS RESEARCH

Early History of Individual Psychotherapy Process Research

Psychotherapy process research can be traced back to the 1930s and Carl Rogers (Gill, Newman, & Redlich, 1954; Gottman & Markman, 1978; Kiesler, 1973; Mahrer, 1985; Russell, 1987; Small & Manthei, 1986). Rogers (1942) is generally credited as the first researcher to seek to identify "moments of movement" (Mahrer, 1985, p. 92). The goal of these early researchers was to find those "moments of movement" in therapy that led to a change of personality or behavior by the client.

Initially, process research methodology tended to study only the therapist's behaviors. This line of research, however, was generally unproductive. It was not until the 1960s that the interaction between therapist and client was examined (Bordin, 1962). This led to gathering a corpus of data that was quite large and methodologically unwieldy. Kiesler's (1973) seminal book on process research reported one study where the "researchers possessed 1,204 hours of tape-recorded therapeutic interaction with twenty-eight patients" (p. 27) and the researchers struggled with the difficulty of reducing the process data to a manageable and analyzable load. During this period, process researchers were still striving to develop methodologies to deal with these types of issues.

Kiesler's (1973) book also followed the practice of dividing process research according to the employment of either direct or indirect measures. Direct measures included coding and rating systems applied by trained judges observing live or transcribed sessions and indirect measures were self-report inventory questionnaires for the patient and therapist. Kiesler (1986), however, in reviewing his earlier work, stated the use of direct research "reflected an implicit value that the perspective of observers who rated the actual behaviors of the participants (the objective environment) was more valid than the subjective environments represented by the experience of the participants" (p. vii). Kiesler (1986) said that this bias was unfair and, indeed, led to some invalid empirical findings.

Kiesler's 1973 book, which was the first attempt to compile the "available tools of process research in psychotherapy between the covers of one book" (Strupp, 1973, p. xv), did revitalize interest in therapy process research. With this interest, new advances and developments were made in process research. One new development was that of "viewing the interaction between therapist and client as a reciprocal social influence process" (Gottman & Markman, 1978, p. 27). This new development, however, raised even more methodological problems (Gottman & Markman, 1978; Kiesler, 1973).

At the heart of these problems was the difficulty of developing methodologically sound process instruments for evaluating the data. It was crucial to adequately represent what was happening in the therapy process with a classification scheme that could be analyzed. The common practice of employing rates or frequencies of a certain type of behavior as a measure of change was problematic both theoretically and statistically (Elliott, 1983; Greenberg, 1982; Greenberg & Pinsof, 1986; Rice & Greenberg, 1984b; Rice & Kerr, 1986; Gottman & Markman, 1978). Gottman and Markman (1978) pointed out that "the use of rates to operationalize process notions is an extremely crude swipe at . . . . a reasonable process relationship" (p. 28).

Additionally, even with the development of a consideration of therapist/client interaction there was an unfortunate reluctance by process researchers to focus on the complex interaction of the many elements of the psycho-therapeutic context, for example, interaction of therapist, client, context, and techniques. Parloff, Waskow, and Wolfe (1978) stated that for a variety of reasons, "researchers [were] usually content to conduct studies focused primarily on one of these interacting elements" (p. 233). Typically, researchers looked only at either the therapist's behavior *or* the client's behavior.

Another problem with process research during this period was the paucity of process-outcome studies. Parloff et al. (1978) noted a limitation of current process research was that there were very few studies relating "patient-therapist relationship dimensions to outcome" (p. 234). Orlinsky and Howard (1978), in addition, reported poor results from the few process-outcome research that had been conducted. One of the many problems that they found in process research at that time was that researchers were not clearly reporting what they were investigating. Orlinsky and Howard suggested that what was needed were better descriptions of the phenomena of the psychotherapeutic process.

Orlinsky and Howard (1978), as well as other authors, also stressed the importance of integrating scientific inquiry with clinical application (Barlow, 1981; Bergin & Strupp, 1972; Elliott, 1983; Luborsky, 1972). They warned that without process-outcome studies that were informative to clinicians, process research will not alter clinicians' practice and they will only "trust their clinical experience and their clinical mentors" (Luborsky, 1972, p. 125).

The Discovery-oriented Intensive Analysis Approach Towards Process Research

In the final chapter of Greenberg and Pinsof's (1986) seminal work, *The Psychotherapeutic Process: A Research Handbook,* Greenberg (1986b) projected some of the future needs of process research. He saw a shift in research away from prediction and towards explanation. Greenberg stated:

> Only when outcome predictions of this type can be explained in terms of the active ingredients of treatment, how change takes place, and when and with whom specific treatments are effective, will psychotherapy research move from a prescientific to a scientific stage of development. (p. 709)

In order to achieve these types of results, Greenberg stated, "It is crucial that more rigorous research to promote these goals be done and more sophisticated procedures be developed to promote this effort" (p. 710).

Greenberg (1986b), like Rice and Greenberg (1984a) earlier, went on to state that what is still important in psychotherapy research is the discovery of phenomena which should "be the primary data of psychotherapy research" (p. 711). Advances will be made through intensive analysis and description of these phenomena and it is only after these phenomena have been reliably described and measured that "the emphasis can shift from description to explanation of phenomena, model building, and finally prediction" (Greenberg, 1986b, p. 712).

Safran, Greenberg, and Rice (1988), two years later, stated that the present needs of process research as expressed by the "leading voices in the psychotherapy field" require "the use of intensive analysis procedures" (p. 1). This is a discovery approach that begins with the labor-intensive process of generating hypotheses from the microanalysis of individual cases.

These authors go on to say that experienced clinicians continually adapt their interventions based on the current needs of their clients. In describing this type of knowledge, they note that "clinical wisdom and the associated skill is referred to as timing" (p. 5). Safran et al. (1988) cite as their central premise that process research needs to articulate systematically the principles guiding this timing. In many ways, process researchers were still looking for those "moments of movement" that Rogers (1942) sought.

Safran et al. (1988) suggest that there are different shifts that go on in the client's psychological state that form the context for the therapist's interventions. The process of therapy is then seen as a chain of suboutcomes that are linked together towards some "ultimate outcome" (p. 5). The methodology for finding these suboutcomes involves delineating them empirically by viewing a few cases intensively.

Thus begins a process of looping back and forth between the intensive observations of actual behavior and the emerging performance model as developed by the researcher. The type of information such a research process could reveal is just recently under investigation. This form of research has potential for impacting the clinician's practice (Safran et al., 1988).

During the 1980s, several books (Greenberg & Pinsof, 1986; Mahrer, 1985; Rice & Greenberg, 1984a), and many papers were published that highlighted this discovery-oriented intensive analysis approach. The following section will discuss the work of a few process researchers who followed this intensive discovery-oriented methodology.

Task analysis. The task analysis research of Rice and Greenberg (1984a, 1984b; Greenberg, 1984) is a research approach that exemplifies the intensive discovery methodology defined by Safran et al. (1988). Task analysis is primarily "an approach in which the components of competence of successful performances are specified in order to understand problem solving" within the therapy session (Greenberg, 1984, p. 127). Rice and Greenberg's (1984b) strategy involves selecting particular episodes and studying the process of those events within their context (rather than sampling randomly for events). These events are selected both on the basis of theory and observation. It is a "rational-empirical" approach in that it is assumed that there are fixed organization features of human behavior that occur across a particular class of situations and which can be studied through rigorous observation and induction.

Though they were looking at the interactional sequence between the client and the therapist, Rice and Greenberg (1984b) were chiefly interested in focusing on the client's responses, as they were looking for "the pattern of the client process" (p. 20). The strategy of task analysis begins with the researcher describing the client's task, specifying the task environment and then looking at both the mental and behavioral process of the client in solving the task.

Following those four steps, the researcher constructs a performance model to represent his or her understanding of how the client resolved the task. This model is then compared to new single-cases of client's resolving tasks. "This is done in an iterataive manner, moving back and forth between idealized and actual performances until a refined proposed model of a resolution performance is built" (Greenberg, 1986a, p. 7).

Interpersonal process recall. Another research design that is representative of the discovery-oriented research methodology involves the application of the interpersonal process recall (IPR) protocol (Bergin & Strupp, 1972; Kiesler, 1973; Elliott, 1983, 1984, 1986; Rice & Greenberg, 1984b). Elliott (1983, 1984, 1986) is currently the most active researcher in IPR. The methodology of IPR is to play back the therapeutic conversation to the participants and to ask them to "remember and describe the momentary experiences and perceptions associated with particular events in the conversation" (Elliott, 1986, p. 503).

Elliott's (1986) use of IPR developed out of the need to construct "contextually sensitive process measures" (p. 506). Through questioning the client and the therapist after playback of the tape, Elliott sought qualitative information to pick up new details of the therapeutic process. Elliott (1984) compares his use of IPR to the task analytic approach noting "that it selects specific therapeutic events for study on the basis of potency and recurrence, subjects them to analyses whose result is the identification of common features" which can be used "as the basis for constructing models of the change process in psychotherapy" (p. 283).

In-therapy change, and client and therapist vocal quality. Two other approaches that follow this intensive discovery-oriented methodology were used by Mahrer (Mahrer, 1985; Mahrer & Nadler, 1986; Mahrer, Dessaulles, Nadler, Gervaize, & Sterner, 1987) and Rice and Kerr (Duncan, Rice, & Butler, 1968; Rice & Kerr, 1986). Both approaches combine being guided by theory and previous research while intensively listening to audiotapes in order to create a classification system for analyzing the significant events in the therapeutic process.

Building on the research that Carl Rogers began, Mahrer (1985) wanted to find "indices of psychotherapeutic movement" (p. 92), or as he calls them, "good moments" in therapy. Mahrer, Dessaulles, Nadler, Gervaize, and Sterner (1987) developed a list of 12 good moments in therapy. Rice and Kerr (1986) developed a classification of vocal patterns indicative of change in the therapeutic process. Both methodologies then relied on trained coders to listen to audiotapes of a session or two (and sometimes read a transcript of those sessions) and code those significant moments.

Mahrer's research tends to focus more on the content of the therapy talk, while Rice and Kerr's research focuses on the paralinguistic features of the conversation. Rice and Kerr (1986) add, however, "that therapy involves not only voice quality but also verbal content and body language" (p. 100). To address this dimension, Rice and Kerr (1986) are beginning to incorporate Elliott's IPR system with their voice quality methodology as a way to study more of the process.

Content, speech act, episode, and relationship. Also emphasizing the issue of measuring more of the multidimensional elements of the therapy process, Greenberg (1986a, 1986b) stressed the need to develop context-sensitive instruments. Greenberg (1986a) noted that the fallacy that "all processes have the same meaning (regardless of context) needs to be dropped" (p. 4). Social meaning is context-dependent. To address the challenge of finding a level of description or unit of analysis that is sensitive to context, he suggests using units of description (from Pearce and Cronen, 1980) that encompass four levels of process. The levels include content, speech act, episode, and relationship.

These four levels are hierarchically arranged in that content, which is what is being talked about without reference to the kind of message being used, is an aspect of the speech act. Speech acts, which involve what one person is doing to another (Austin, 1975), can be viewed in the context of the type of episode in which they occur. Episodes are communicative patterns, which have distinct openings and closing sequences that are understood within the context of the relationship in which they occur. The relationship level describes "particular qualities that people attribute to the ongoing relationship" (Greenberg, 1986b, p. 715). Greenberg (1986b) goes on to suggest what is needed are a battery of instruments that can describe the different levels in the hierarchy so that the researcher can more clearly describe the meaning of the ongoing actions of both the client and the therapist.

FAMILY THERAPY PROCESS RESEARCH

Two Major Reviews of Family Therapy Process Research

Pinsof (1981) wrote the first major review of process research in family therapy. His chapter, in Gurman and Kniskern's (1981) *Handbook of Fam-*

ily Therapy, pointed out the need for process research in the family therapy field. Pinsof stated that "the field of family therapy process research has just been born" (p. 700) and "a clear and consistent body of knowledge (both substantive and methodological) has not yet emerged" (p. 738).

Indeed, Gurman and Kniskern's (1978) chapter on research on marital and family therapy focused only on outcome research and not process research. Pinsof (1981) cited three reasons for the dearth of family therapy process research. These reasons include the difficulty of the task, the lack of good microtherapy theory, and the fact that process researchers in general have been individually oriented and have ignored family therapy as a new theoretical orientation.

Pinsof went on to state:

> This scientific isolation has retarded the speed with which the knowledge and skill offered by the field of psychotherapy research have infused the family therapy field. Simultaneously, it has permitted general psychotherapy researchers to remain enmeshed within a predominantly individual psychotherapy research paradigm. (p. 701)

Pinsof noted that most of the family therapy process research tended to use coding systems of either the therapist's or client's behavior. Pinsof's review of research revealed that neither "process research focusing on the behavior of the family therapist" (p. 714) nor "the research on the behavior of family members" (p. 719) in family therapy had produced a clear or consistent body of substantive findings. The few studies that were an exception to this either/or dichotomy tended to be broad systems for analyzing the structure of human interaction rather than research designed specifically for psychotherapy.

An example of this type of research, which looked at both the client and therapist, was Scheflen's (1973) study which employed a context analytical methodology. Scheflen eschewed theoretical assumptions and experimental design and applied an ethnographic, "intensive, detailed description of every discernable . . . . behavior . . . . of every individual within" the group setting (Pinsof, 1981, p. 721).

Scheflen's (1973) method was not to impose a coding system upon the data, but rather, to discover categories via observing particular transactions. Pinsof (1981) reported that the benefit of Scheflen's approach is that it is "the least reductionistic process analysis method" as "it does minimal violence to the integrity and uniqueness of a given transaction" (p. 722). Its deficit, however, "is the complexity and sophistication of the method" (p. 722) and its inability to be applied across different psychotherapeutic situations.

Pinsof (1981) characterized family therapy process research up to that time as exploratory. In discussing methodological issues, Pinsof cited Kiesler's (1973) chapter on methodology as a good companion to his chapter. Pinsof noted, however, that the major limitation of Kiesler's chapter is that it was written from an individual epistemological perspective. Pinsof asserted that in developing methodologies for family therapy process research the current process research methodology of individually oriented psychotherapy must be changed or expanded to accommodate the unique theoretical features of family therapy.

One of the most important issues that family therapy process researchers faced during this period (1970s) was blending methodology with the family therapy paradigm. Family therapy rested "on a conceptual foundation derived from general systems theory" and "the implications of this perspective for psychotherapy research (both process and outcome) have hardly been explored" (Pinsof, 1981, pp. 726–727). Pinsof stated "that in selecting variables and in choosing or creating measurement systems, the researcher should be cognizant of the extent to which they accommodate the unique theoretical and pragmatic realities of family therapy" (p. 732).

By the mid-1980s process research was slowly beginning to come into its own. Some of the distinctions between individual psychotherapy process research and family therapy process research were becoming blurred. Researchers from the two therapy paradigms were combining efforts in conducting research and in developing methodologies. Rice and Greenberg (1984a) edited a book highlighting current discovery-oriented process research. In 1986 two major reviews of process research were published (Greenberg & Pinsof, 1986; Gurman et al., 1986). However, a major issue in family therapy process research continued to be the search for methodologies that could examine data and reflect the circular, cybernetic epistemology of family therapy (Gurman et al., 1986).

Gurman et al. (1986) point out that the new epistemology of family therapy based on cybernetics and systems theory challenges traditional research. With circular causality, there is no distinction between dependent and independent variables. Gurman et al. (1986) noted, however, that the new epistemology, while different from the traditional linear approach of research, has not offered an alterative methodology. Units of analysis are incomplete and this perspective requires that researchers "look at how these parts are connected, and this is a commitment to process as well as structure" (Segal & Bavelas, 1983, p. 67).

Therefore, Gurman et al. (1986) recommend continuing research along more traditional lines. They do warn, though, of the dangers of stifling the "emergence of alternative methods of systematically coming to 'know' the mechanisms of change in family therapy" (p. 569). For this reason they do encourage research that is discovery-oriented.

This discovery-oriented research, or "new process perspective" (Gurman et al., 1986) is directly connected to the discovery-oriented intensive analysis approach discussed earlier. Gurman et al. stated that this new process perspective does derive "from family therapy theory and represents a significant contribution from the family therapy field to the general field of psychotherapy research" (p. 596). The authors suggest that progress in the process analysis task of family therapy will be slow in coming as researchers need to "deal with all the problems involved with individual therapy process research as well as those unique to the family therapy context" (p. 597).

One major gap in the family therapy field that Gurman et al. point to is the lack of attention paid to nonverbal behaviors. They note that "no one in the field has developed and implemented an empirical and quantitative methodology for studying paralinguistic . . . . and kinesic . . . . behaviors" (p. 598). The authors state that the initial work done by Scheflen (1973) and Birdwhistle (1970) in this area has not been pursued or developed by others in the family therapy field.

Gurman et al. (1986) suggest that the leading edge of family therapy process research should follow the new process perspective. This approach stresses the importance for researchers to determine "the salient variables" and the "instruments to measure the salient variables, and research strategies that will uncover the links" that exist in practice (p. 599). These authors point out the need for process research to focus on "change episodes" within the therapy process: "This approach requires the identification of a specific, clinically significant occurrence within a treatment session" (p. 600).

Recommendations of Gurman et al. (1986) included the importance of making research relevant to the clinician. "If psychotherapy research, whatever its multiple motivations, does not have a meaningful impact on practicing clinicians, its continued pursuit must be seriously questioned" (p. 612). They also stated that "We believe that the study of common effective elements and mechanisms of change in family therapy, irrespective of their 'parent' schools of thought is essential to further conceptual and clinical development in the field" (p. 613).

State of the art of family therapy process research. Many of these sentiments are shared by other leading process researchers in the family therapy field. Wynne's (1988a) edited book, *The State of the Art in Family Therapy Research: Controversies and Recommendations,* is the most recent major work that explores family therapy research (both process and outcome). This book evolved out of a 1984 workshop that brought together 19 leading family therapists/researchers with staff from the National Institute of Mental Health. Following are some of the key points made by the different researchers who contributed to Wynne's book.

Wynne (1988c), in his overview of the book/conference, stated that the participants of the conference agreed that emphasis should be towards exploratory, discovery-oriented, hypothesis-generating research. He also added that "family therapy research should be theory-based and theory-driven" (p. 250). Wynne, however, also said that family therapy research should follow a more traditional methodology. While others (Auerswald, 1988; Pinsof, 1988; Stanton, 1988; Steier, 1988) agreed with the importance of integrating theory with research, there was some question regarding the degree to which researchers should (or, can) incorporate a systemic epistemology in their methodologies.

Stanton (1988), while agreeing with the need to understand the conceptual and operational basis for making clinical decisions, also challenged the notion that there is an absolute reality that can be measured objectively. Auerswald (1988) believed "that research based in this epistemologically altered reality will be, in the end, more generically useful than research that is now being done" (p. 56).

Steier (1988) called for "the adoption of a paradigm more consistent with a cybernetic-perspective, which . . . . underlies the cyclical nature of any research program concerned with social interventions" (pp. 232–233). The difficulty with this position, that Wynne (1988c) points out, is that "it is not always clear how some formulations of family systems theory and ecosystemic theory can in fact be connected to clinical observations" (p. 250). This matches with the position of Gurman et al. (1986), stated earlier, of employing research that follows traditional lines until new methodologies that are sensitive to cybernetic, systemic interactions can be developed.

Another aspect of research that the authors of the book agreed upon is that "The researcher, often inaccurately viewed as an 'independent' evaluator, helps shape the research system that constitutes still another observing system" (Wynne, 1988c, p. 254). Steier (1988) suggests that researchers use the data collection process as part of the research methodology. Steier stated, "We must include . . . . the study of the observing system—the research/therapy system observing itself in the act of performing an intervention" (p. 234).

Wynne (1988b) observed that investigators should do research that brings in the multiple perspectives of the family, the therapist, the family/therapist system, and the researcher. Anderson (1988) suggests that in order to gather these multilevel measurements, "we need strategies that include measures of perception and behavior" (p. 86). Pinsof (1988) adds that self-reports should be included in process research in order to provide multiple perspectives as well as to help link process with outcome. Pinsof also suggests that researchers should look for "small-o" outcomes that reflect proximal changes, or changes that occur in the session hour and reflect smaller units of process-outcome linkages.

Gaps in family therapy process research. In summarizing the above views, it can be seen that family therapy process research is struggling between following the research methodologies of an individually oriented linear paradigm or following research consistent with the cybernetic, systemic paradigm. While the "new process perspective" of individual psychotherapy does offer family therapy researchers new methodologies, these methods also have their limitations for family therapy theory. The tension between these two approaches exposes one of the major gaps in the field. As Gurman et al. (1986) stated:

> Family therapy not only represents an additive complication, but actually creates a new interpersonal gestalt that is not adequately addressed by the methods, procedures, and designs of individual therapy process research. The process analysis task in family therapy is more difficult and progress will of necessity be slower, particularly during these early years of its development. (p. 597)

This leads to the question of how researchers will define and explore those issues relevant to the cybernetic, systemic paradigm of family therapy (e.g., Keeney, 1982, Pinsof, 1988; Stanton, 1988; Steier, 1988). Bateson (1977) stated, "The new science will form around profoundly non-physical ideas: the nature of the relation between name and that which is named, the nature of recursive systems, and the nature of difference" (p. 337). Keeney (1982) pointed out that "pattern and form have no 'realness,' are not subject to quantification, and cannot be discussed as though they were 'things' influenced by the interplay of force, power, and energy" (p. 162).

The views of Bateson (1972, 1977, 1979), Keeney (1982, 1983, personal communication, 1987), Steier (1985, 1988, personal communication, January 16, 1990) and others leads to the importance of developing research tools that are sensitive to context and pattern. Schwartzman (1984) pointed out that the predicament for family therapy process researchers is "that family interactional research has largely ceased to pursue questions of meaning and pattern in the quest for methodological rigor" (p. 230).

Areas in which there continues to be a need for further investigation by family therapy researchers include: exploring the interactive talk of the clients *and* the therapist; studying nonverbal, or paralinguistic features of the therapy talk; finding a common language of change irrespective of the parent school of therapy; and working with the issue of the observer as helping to shape the research system. Finding methodologies which can explore these gaps will be valuable to the family therapy profession in that not only will cybernetic, systemic theory be developed and clarified, but practical applications for clinicians can be learned. Providing clinicians with context-sensitive instruments and information regarding patterns of interaction can also help bridge the gap between researchers and clinicians (Andreozzi, 1985; Steier, 1985).

Wynne (1988c) also stresses the importance of closing these gaps as he states:

> It seems timely for the family therapy field to reconsider and reassess its missions, it conceptual base, and its mode of relating to families. In this process of self-scrutiny, family therapy research should contribute. Collaboration between family clinicians and researchers is essential in setting priorities for family therapy research that optimally will be: valued by families, significant to practitioners, credible to health care policymaking and funding organizations, methodologically feasible, and conceptually interesting and/or provocative. (p. 264)

ETHNOMETHODOLOGY AND CONVERSATION ANALYSIS

Ethnomethodology

Harold Garfinkel is considered the father of ethnomethodology. Garfinkel's (1967) book elucidated a method for studying (ology) and describing ordinary people's (ethno) methods of practical reasoning. Garfinkel's methods clearly revealed "the extent to which the shared nature of ordinary understandings is dependent on the joint application of shared methods of reasoning" (Heritage, 1988, p. 128). Pomerantz and Atkinson (1984) reported that Garfinkel was recommending:

> a "folk" methodology comprising a range of "seen but unnoticed" procedures or practices that make it possible for persons to analyse, make sense of, and produce recognizable social activities, but which have remained largely unexplicated by social researchers. (p. 286)

Parsons' scientific methodology. To understand what Garfinkel was accomplishing, it is important to consider the historical context within which he was working. Garfinkel, a sociologist, was a student of Talcot Parsons at Harvard University in the 1940s. Parsons' influence on sociology was toward developing theoretical concepts built around the subjective experience of social actors. This created an emphasis on building conceptual abstractions to explain the social sciences. Parsons' understanding of a person's actions was in terms "of concepts which were almost wholly 'external' to the point of view of the actor" (Heritage, 1984, p. 22). Action was analyzed as the product of causal processes, which, while "operating in the minds of the actors, were all but inaccessible to them and, hence, uncontrollable by them" (Heritage, 1984, p. 22).

Garfinkel's ethnomethodology. Garfinkel (1967) disagreed with Parsons' scientific methodology, which strived to understand a person's actions objectively, looking for internal norms that regulated social activities. Garfinkel thought it crucial to consider "the common-sense world in which ordinary actors choose courses of action on the basis of detailed practical considerations and judgements which are intelligible and accountable to others" (Heritage, 1984, p. 34). He believed that to successfully analyze social action it is necessary to consider the judgements (as expressed through their communicative interactions) of the participants themselves.

Garfinkel's methodology is "primarily descriptive and naturalistic rather than explanatory or experimental" (Heritage, 1988, p. 127). Through various projects, such as listening to the talk of jurors making decisions, Garfinkel (1967) sought to learn the reasoning procedures of ordinary people. Garfinkel (1967) was interested in the jurors' construction of their social reality.

Jurors have no training and no technical skills with which to reach and agree upon their important decisions, and yet they accomplish their task in often very sophisticated manners. Under these circumstances, what makes them jurors? Garfinkel (1967) saw the jurors activities "as a method of social inquiry" (p. 104) in which to understand and make sense of what they had heard during the course of the trial. Schwartz and Jacobs (1979) stated that if these jurors "had been social scientists, we would say that they were using and discussing 'methodology' " (p. 210). Garfinkel became interested in how talk, or the language of various groups of people, helped to construct particular social institutions.

In his work Garfinkel reversed the tradition of theorizing that norms guide human conduct. From his perspective, "the common norms, rather than regulating conduct in pre-defined scenes of action, are instead reflexively constitutive of the activities and unfolding circumstances to which they are applied" (Heritage, 1984, p. 109). In other words, rather than defining a conceptual abstraction of the underlying rules that organize human interaction, Garfinkel posed that the contextual actions themselves are what create the rules. Garfinkel's (1967) methodology differs from traditional social science research in that rather than doing causal or deterministic theorizing, "ethnomethodology research sets out to describe how human behaviour works, rather than to explain why some particular type of behavior occurs" (Pomerantz & Atkinson, 1984, p. 287).

Garfinkel (1967) stated "that the activities whereby members produce and manage settings of organized everyday affairs are identical with members' procedures for making those settings 'account-able' " and "the 'reflexive,' or 'incarnate' character of accounting practices and accounts" (p. 1) are the methods used to understand these activities. This challenges the traditional view of outside observers being able to theorize about what is *really* happening in social interactions.

Rather, understanding is incarnate within the contextual activity itself. "It is precisely through the reflexive accountability of action that ordinary actors find themselves in a world of practical actions having the property that whatever they do will be intelligible and accountable" as a way of maintaining "some order of activity" (Heritage, 1984, p. 110). This belief led to a major shift in sociological methodology in that it transformed the notion of perceiving rules as regulative. Instead, rules started to be seen as constitutive of the interactive context itself.

In order to understand the development and foundation of conversation analysis, several other points made by Garfinkel need to be elaborated. Garfinkel's (1967) recommendations or "policies" for using the ethnomethodological approach covered five main points. The first point is that while any setting can be analyzed to discover how the participants' actions affect their choices, the characteristics of these actions are "located within the setting because they are the product of actions which are produced within it" (Heritage, 1984, p. 134). It is these actions alone which accomplish the organizational work through which the setting is continuously produced.

The second point is that to understand how social interactions maintain their cohesion and continuity, it is necessary to see how the organizational rules of interaction are contingently produced through practical action and applied in that context. This leads to Garfinkel's third point that it is not satisfactory to invoke rules that are not indexed within the context itself. Tyler (1978) states that indexical expressions are so named "because they 'index' or 'stand' for elements of their context" (p. 384). Rules should not be referenced to external or independent events, but they should be grounded in the characteristics of the setting as talked about by the settings' participants.

The fourth point is that any social setting can be viewed as a self-organizing system. "Any setting organizes its activities to make its properties as an organized environment of practical activities detectable, countable, recordable, reportable, tell-a-story-aboutable, analyzable-in short, accountable" (Garfinkel, 1967, p. 33). The final point that Garfinkel makes is that members of a setting are continuously engaged in creating and making sense out of their circumstances and the constituent actions of these circumstances. Therefore, validity in this methodology follows from using the same criteria that the participants themselves use in their context.

These five points that Garfinkel (1967) highlighted provided him with a methodology to study and analyze the discourse of people in various settings. As Heritage (1984) points out, Garfinkel stressed that understanding language is not " 'cracking a cosmic code' which contains a set of pre-established descriptive terms combined . . . . to yield sentence meaning which express propositions about the world" (p. 139). Rather, understanding language is "understanding actions—utterances—which are constructively interpreted in relation to their contexts" (p. 139).

Through analysis of the participants' discourse, their descriptions can be viewed as "indexical" and thereby understood in reference to where and when they occurred. Like other actions, descriptions are also "reflexive" in that they maintain or alter the sense of meaning of the activities through the unfolding circumstances in which they occur. Descriptions are therefore not disembodied commentaries on states of affairs, but rather, in the manner that they do make reference to states of affairs and do "occur in particular interactional and situational contexts, they will unavoidably be understood as actions which are chosen and consequential" (Heritage, 1984, p. 140).

Conversation Analysis

The origins of conversation analysis can be traced to the early 1970s and the works of Harvey Sacks and his collaborators Emmanuel Schegloff and Gail Jefferson (Heritage, 1984; Potter & Wetherell, 1987). Conversation analysis is an outgrowth of ethnomethodology (Sacks and Garfinkel did work together), and is an approach that "many ethnomethodologists have adopted" (Potter & Wetherell, 1987, p. 30) as an analytic strategy in order to work from a stronger empirical basis.

Sacks (1987) stated:

> When I started to do research in sociology I figured that sociology could not be an actual science unless it was able to handle the details of actual events, handle them formally, and in the first instance be informative about them in the direct ways in which primitive sciences tend to be informative, that is, that anyone else can go and see whether what was said is so. And that is a tremendous control on seeing whether one is learning anything. So the question was, could there be some way that sociology could hope to deal with the details of actual events, formally and informatively? . . . I wanted to locate some set of materials that would permit a test. (p. 26)

In developing this approach, Sacks (1987) worked with tape recordings because "I could study it again and again" and "because other people could look at what I had studied and make of it what they could, if, for example they wanted to disagree with me" (p. 26). Levinson (1983) stated that conversation analysis "is a rigorously empirical approach which avoids premature theory construction" and whose methods are essentially inductive in that a "search is made for recurring patterns across many records of naturally occurring conversations (pp. 286–287).

Conversation analysis is an approach which investigates "the normative structures of reasoning which are involved in understanding and producing courses of intelligible interaction" (Heritage, 1988, p. 128). Its objective "is to describe the procedures by which speakers produce their own behaviour and understand and deal with the behaviour of others" (Heritage, 1988, p. 128). Conversation analysis is concerned with empirical data. The analysis is strongly data-driven, guided by the phenomena which appear in the data of interaction.

Conversation analysis examines the paralinguistic features of the talk as well as the structural sequencing of the various turn-takings in the conversation. This research is primarily concerned with the different manner in which "utterances accomplish particular actions by virtue of their placement and participation with sequences of actions" (Heritage, 1984, p. 245). The primary units of analysis are the sequences and turns within sequences (as well as the paralinguistic features of the talk). There is "a strong bias against a priori speculation about the orientations and motives of speakers and in favour of detailed examination of conversationalists' actual action" (Heritage, 1984, p. 243).

Tyler (1978) noted that "language is . . . . a phenomenon of the social group rather than individual psychology" (p. 6). Conversation analysis provides a method to discover how people create various social institutions. Through the microanalysis of conversation, context can be seen "as something endogenously generated within the talk of the participants and, indeed, as something created in and through that talk" (Heritage, 1984, p. 283). Through the local sequences of discourse, various social institutions (courtrooms, classrooms, therapy offices) are talked into being.

Heritage (1984) closes his book on Garfinkel, ethnomethodology and conversation analysis with the following:

> The common theme of these enterprises has been (Garfinkel's) attempt to come more directly into contact with the raw data of human experience and conduct by stripping away the innumerable theoretical and methodological barriers which imperceptibly interpose themselves between observers and organizationally significant features of social activity. . . . . The research of the past twenty years or so has resulted in the creation of the sociological equivalent of the microscope. . . . . The instrument has been built: the challenge is to start working with it. (p. 311)

Filling the Gap

As has been seen, family therapy process research is struggling between being consistent with a cybernetic, systemic paradigm ("the new epistemology"; Gurman et al., 1986) and following the traditional research methodologies of an individual oriented, linear paradigm. As Wynne (1988c) stated, "family therapists have long agreed that this field should be regarded as an approach or a paradigm, and not just another treatment modality" (p. 250). Wynne, however, goes on to say that the "major methodological/conceptual difficulty for family therapy research is "how to carry out empirical research with diverse, individualized information and not reductionistically drain it of clinical, relational 'juice' " (p. 254).

While Gurman et al. (1986), and many of the authors of Wynne's (1988a) edited book support the move towards intensive, discovery-oriented research, or the new process perspective as it is referred to, Gurman et al. (1986) also stressed the need not to stifle the "emergence of alternative methods of systematically coming to 'know' the mechanisms of change in family therapy" (p. 569).

Such a method of knowing change is the ethnomethodological approach of conversation analysis. Given that a major concern of family therapy process researchers is to avoid stripping events from their context through a reductionistic approach, conversation analysis strives to preserve the contextual integrity of the conversation. As pointed out by Heritage (1984), three fundamental assumptions of conversation analysis are:

> 1) interaction is structurally organized, 2) contributions to interaction are contextually organized and 3) these two properties inhere in the details of interaction so that no order of detail can be dismissed, a priori, as disorderly, accidental or irrelevant. (p. 241)

From this perspective, a speaker's communication can be described as doubly contextual in that it is both context-shaped and context-renewing. Each speaker's action is context-shaped in that its meaning can only be understood in reference to the context in which it is spoken. Speakers' actions are also context-renewing as the current episode of talk then helps to contribute to the framework of the developing context.

The context of communication interaction becomes part of the weave that conversation analysts explore. Conversation analysis works very closely with the empirical data (recording and verbatim transcripts) to see how the participants themselves create and use their context. Speakers are very sensitive to the sequencing of the talk. Schegloff and Sacks (1973) stated:

> by an adjacently produced second, a speaker can show that he understood what a prior aimed at, and that he is willing to go along with that. Also, by virtue of the occurrence of an adjacently produced second, the doer of a first can see that what he intended was indeed understood and that it was or was not accepted. . . . It is then through the use of adjacent positioning that ap-

preciations, failures, corrections et cetera can themselves be understandably attempted. (pp. 297–298)

The importance of sequential turn taking in conversation follows from Garfinkel's ideas of the indexical and reflexive nature of communication. Patterns of meanings are indexed to events in the context. Also, "both the instance and the underlying pattern are reflexively determined; knowledge about the underlying pattern being used as a means for identifying the instance, and the instance being used to determine the pattern" (Tyler, 1978, p. 397).

This matches with Steier's (1988) position that it is important to include contextual change and the sequences of change, or patterns over time, as a relevant factor in family therapy process research. As Steier (1988) states, "the importance of reflexivity in sensemaking of family therapy research is key" (p. 233) to this process.

The ethnomethodological approach of conversation analysis can prove to be a resource for filling the gap in family therapy process research. Conversation analysis is a naturalistic approach that is nondisruptive to the conversations that it explores. Like Scheflen's (1973) approach mentioned above, it is context sensitive and maintains the integrity of the therapeutic process. It is a system that can be used by many different schools of therapy, regardless of their orientation.

Conversation analysis is also sensitive to the nuances of the new epistemology of family therapy. It is sensitive to observing events from a cybernetic orientation in that it notes the sequences of talk as they are recursively, or reflexively connected within the context of the conversation. The back-and-forth feedback of turn taking in conversation is a crucial element in the construction of various contexts.

As Garfinkel (1967) stated, "The method consists of treating an actual appearance as 'the document of,' as 'pointing to,' as 'standing on behalf of' a presupposed underlying pattern" (p. 78). He goes on to say that "not only is the underlying pattern derived from its individual documentary evidences, but the individual documentary evidences, in their turn, are interpreted on the basis of 'what is known' about the underlying pattern. Each is used to elaborate the other" (p. 78). This view is similar to a cybernetic perspective in that the various patterns of talk are recursively connected and contextually created.

Through examining the turn-taking sequences and the paralinguistic features of the talk, conversation analysts seek to identify patterns of interactional information. This fits in well with Bateson's (1972, 1977, 1979) ideas. Schwartzman (1984), in discussing Bateson's ideas, said that "in a cybernetic epistemology, mental process, ideas, communication, organization, differentiation, pattern, and so on, are matters of form rather than substance" (p. 225).

Ethnomethodology is also consistent with the new epistemology in terms of abandoning "representation as the central concept for understanding cognitive mechanisms" (Varela, 1989, p. 16). As stated earlier, Garfinkel reversed the social science tradition of theorizing that norms guide human conduct. Garfinkel instead saw that "the common norms, rather than regulating conduct in pre-defined scenes of action, are instead reflexively constitutive of the activities and unfolding circumstances to which they are applied" (Heritage, 1984, p. 109). Heritage (1984), paraphrasing Garfinkel, states that "the meaning of the words is not ordained by some preexisting agreement on correspondences between world and objects. Instead, it remains to be actively and constructively made out" (p. 310).

As Gurman et al. (1986) pointed out, the cutting edge of family therapy process research is the new process perspective of the intensive, discovery-oriented approach. Conversation analysis provides a method of analysis that includes this approach as well as an exploration of the intricacies of the interactive context. Conversation analysis is able to examine the episodes of task analysis (Rice & Greenberg, 1984a) in a manner that looks at *all* the participants in the changing interactions.

Indeed, conversation analysis is able to study any social activity without needing to artifically set up a task environment. Conversation analysis is able to explore different situations in a naturalistic, nonobtrusive manner. This methodology can incorporate the interpersonal process recall system of Elliott (1986) in a style that is context-sensitive as it examines how the participants' talk is used to construct key moments in therapy. Conversation analysis is useful for locating these moments of change (Mahrer et al., 1987). This approach is also sensitive to the paralinguistic characteristics of communication (Rice & Kerr, 1986). Greenberg's (1986a, 1986b) ideas regarding the hierarchic levels of speech acts, episodes, and relationship also are easily incorporated within this form of analysis of a conversation. Conversation analysis is also capable of studying small-o outcomes in the therapy process (Pinsof, 1988).

This methodological approach satisfies the criteria of Segal and Bavelas (1983) in that the units of analysis do consider how parts are connected and there is a commitment to process as well as structure. Also, this methodology is sensitive to the notion that the researcher/observer is part of the system (Steier, 1988; Wynne, 1988c), and therefore, the researcher clearly lays out his/her empirical data (transcripts) for all to see (Sacks, 1987). This allows each reader the opportunity to draw his/her own conclusions about the analysis presented. Lastly, this approach generates information that is valuable to the clinician and meets the concerns of Gurman et al. (1986) and Wynne (1988c) that research should be relevant to clinical practice.

The intensive microanalysis of conversation that conversation analysts employ in their ethnomethodological approach provides an important methodology for family therapy researchers. This approach is not offered to replace current methodologies and technologies, but rather, to augment the capabilities of researchers. Conversation analysis can help to develop the microtherapy theory that is currently needed in the profession.

As Pinsof (1986) stated, "by and large the field of psychotherapy, and the family therapy field in particular, lacks an explicit, specific, and behaviorally focused micro-theory" (p. 222). The rigorous application of conversation analysis can help develop that microtheory as well as achieve success as a methodology appropriate for research of systemic family therapy. Chapter Three explicates the methodology and procedures of conversation analysis that will be employed in the analysis of the therapy session under investigation.

Chapter 3

Methodology and Procedures

This chapter begins with a presentation of several features of the ethnomethodological and conversation analytic approaches that mark them as different from traditional research methodologies. Ethnomethodology is the class of methodologies which studies the participants' (of a particular context) own "methods of production and interpretation of social interaction" (Levinson, 1983, p. 295). Conversation analysis is a particular type of ethnomethodology that is "a rigorous empirical approach" which is "essentially inductive" (Levinson, 1983, pp. 286–287) and focuses on the microanalysis of the conversation.

The scientific validity of the ethnomethodological and conversation analytic approaches will then be presented through the use of exemplars which either support or do not support a particular theoretical position. Also, the complementary relationship between the ethnomethodological and conversation analytic approaches and the methodological approach of experimentation will be highlighted.

The second part of the chapter presents the purpose of this study. Following this, the procedures used in this study will be delineated. The four steps (selection of a therapeutic session, recording, transcription, and analysis) used in the research methodology will be described and the reflexive nature of these steps will be pointed out. Hopper and Koch (1986) call these the "un-steps" as the researcher almost does all four steps at once. Thus, analysis begins with the very first step of research. Finally, a detailed example will be provided in order to further clarify the analytic procedures of this approach.

METHODS

Ethnomethodology

Garfinkel's (1967) ethnomethodological approach is concerned with understanding institutionalized patterns of social relations through the "analysis of how the actors come to share a common appraisal of their empirical circumstances and, ultimately, a common world" (Heritage, 1984, p. 305). In other words, ethnomethodology is a method that can examine different social contexts, for example, a jury, a therapy session, a crisis hotline through examining the participants' own methods of understanding their social situation. In the case of a therapy session, this would lead to an understanding of how the therapist and the clients, together, create and maintain the institutionalized structure called "a therapy session."

As seen in Chapter Two, this approach, which rejects a view of language as merely a representational activity, treats language as an active process which helps to construct these different social institutions. Language serves a performative function which is understood through realizing the meanings and actions produced by the spoken words (Austin, 1975). As Heritage (1984) states:

> Far from being a rigid framework for the transmission of representations between actors, language is an elastic medium for the performance of actions, and the understanding of utterances must necessarily involve the same range of methodic contextual considerations as the understanding of any other form of action. (p. 310)

Language, therefore, is a performative action that both constructs and maintains varying social contexts. In order to understand these various social contexts, one must examine the very talk itself.

This methodological approach has followed different forms of analysis than traditional social science research. Rather than quantifying and averaging various classifications of a phenomenon, ethnomethodological approaches work directly with the empirical data in a qualitative (or descriptive) manner. The emphasis is on working directly with the participants' language and the participants' own understanding of their social context.

As Heritage (1984) points out, Garfinkel's ethnomethodology enabled researchers to explore "the gap in social science literature on occupations" which "consists of all the missing descriptions of what occupational activities consist of and all the missing analyses of how the practitioners manage the tasks" (p. 299). The therapy session is an example of an unstudied occupational activity (Buttny, 1990).

An example of this methodology was incorporated by Gilbert and Mulkay (1984), who, in their classic study, examined the discourse (conversations) of biochemistry scientists in order to understand how the scientists' accounts of action and belief influenced their scientific endeavors. This study revealed, among other things, that the scientists had two interpretive repertoires, the empiricist repertoire and the contingent repertoire, for understanding their scientific findings.

These two styles differed in that the empiricist style followed formal research logic while the contingent repertoire was influenced by factors outside the realm of empirical phenomena. In other words, the biochemists' reports of their findings were not simply controlled by invariable methodological constraints, but were significantly influenced by the scientist's interactive social context.

Gilbert and Mulkay's (1984) findings are significant in that they point out the relevance of ethnomethodological and conversation analytic approaches which are able to study a domain different than what traditional scientific methodology explores, that is, interactions of experimental subjects (Potter & Wetherell, 1987). To repeat, ethnomethodology explores the gaps in the social science literature by providing an approach that describes the processes of how practitioners manage their various occupational tasks. "Ordinary activities are thus examined for the ways in which they exhibit accountably competent work practices as viewed by practitioners" (Heritage, 1984, p. 302). This approach is different than the approach of traditional research methodologies. To further clarify the distinctions between these research paradigms, it will be useful to look at conversation analytic methodology.

Conversation Analysis

Sacks (1987) states that "ethnomethodology/conversation analysis" exists as "a domain of research . . . . that is not part of any other established science" (p. 21) (from an edited chapter of collected lecture notes written between 1964 and 1971). Sacks (1987) noted that typical research tends to first construct hypothetical propositions before empirically testing these explanations. Indeed, this approach is typified by Kerlinger's (1973) definition of scientific research as the "systematic, controlled, empirical, and critical investigation of hypothetical propositions about the presumed relations among natural phenomena" (p. 11).

Conversation analysis follows a different approach. Observations are used as the basis for theorizing. It follows an inductive methodology and it "is a rigorously empirical approach which avoids premature theory construction" (Levinson, 1983, p. 287). "Therefore," as Sacks (1987) put forth, "the kind of phenomena I deal with are always transcriptions of actual occurrences in their actual sequence" (p. 25). In this manner, any reader can verify the analysis in his/her own way, "and that is a tremendous control on seeing whether one is learning anything" (p. 26).

Levinson (1983) also points out that "for each substantive claim, the methodology employed in CA [conversation analysis] requires evidence not only that some aspect of conversation *can* be viewed in the way suggested, but that it actually is so conceived by the participants producing it" (pp. 318–319). This documentation of the participants' talk provides "us a way of avoiding the indefinitely extendable and unverifiable categorization and speculation of actors' intents (Levinson, 1983, p. 319). Heritage (1988) expresses this as "the objective . . . to describe the procedures by which speakers produce their own behaviour and understand and deal with the behaviour of others" (p. 128).

Pomerantz and Atkinson (1984) state that there are three central points common to both ethnomethodological and conversation analytic research. The first point is that "the main focus should be on how participants themselves produce and interpret each other's actions" (p. 286). The second point is that the researcher must treat *all* the interactional empirical data as unique and different and thus worthy of serious analytic attention. The third element is the preference of working "with naturally occurring interactions, rather than those associated with experimental situations" (p. 287).

Scientific validity of conversation analytic research.

Conversation analysis offers a systematic, ultraempirical procedure for analyzing data. It is systematic in that it follows a rigorous procedure of repeated listening to recordings towards developing the transcription of the conversation. Conversation analysis is empirical in that it employs the naturalistic phenomenon itself, that is, the talk, as the corpus of study. The transcriptions are painstakingly detailed in providing a notation for representing the paralinguistic features of the talk (see Appendix A).

The conversation analyst repeatedly listens to the recorded data and the details of the transcription are continually updated. Information is not discarded by the conversation analyst as the investigator does not know early in the project which details are important.

> Rather, they take pains to re-present data richly. Conversation-analytic data reductions occur late in inquiry, and their results appear in choices of exemplars, and specifications of their details in prose description. (Hopper, 1988, p. 57)

The conversation analyst thus strives to describe what is universally the case.

One method that conversation analysts employ to support scholarly claims is the use of exemplars (Hopper, 1988). Exemplars are detailed examples which demonstrate the validity of a particular theoretical position. Conversation analysts' research reports provide examples of the "winnowing" process that the researcher, without advance knowledge, goes through towards discovering patterns via "repeated exposure to recordings and transcriptions" (Hopper, 1988, p. 54). Falsification is analyzed "by testing descriptions against the details of each new instance" (Hopper, 1988, p. 56). Thus, deviant cases are sought to indicate where established patterns are departed from, "and showing the ways in which the participants, through their actions, orient to these departures" (Heritage, 1988, p. 131).

Conversation analysts often work with data from one source. Conversation analysis stresses descriptive specification of a phenomenon rather than number of examples. Therefore, as Hopper (1988) states:

> If scholars cannot locate a counter-example to a description, a single instance may suffice for reporting it. What would 30 instances add to the descriptions of telephone openings that are available in [two instances cited earlier in Hopper's paper]? The conversation analyst's art includes examining a number of instances in the context of discovery, but reporting only a few of these in scientific essays, accompanying each reported case with detailed description. (p. 57)

Exemplars of the transcript are also provided in the research report so that the reader can assess the data and conclusions for him/herself. The researcher/reader can also replicate or repudiate the findings through seeking different exemplars.

The reliability of the conversation analytic approach also can be approached through the use of exemplars. Validity is tested within the conversational context by tracking how the participants themselves make sense of their talk and comparing exemplars against other exemplars. As Hopper (1988) stated, falsification is revealed "by testing descriptions against the details of each new instance" (p. 56). Reliability is achieved through comparing exemplars from one context, with exemplars from other conversational contexts. As Jacobs and Jackson state (1989) state:

> *Prima facie* evidence for the correctness of any analysis is the display of clear-cut, obvious examples. If the analyst's intuitions are somehow idiosyncratic or peculiar, the descriptions will not resonate with the intuitions of the reader. They will not be clearly recognizable to the reader. Where such cases cannot be displayed, we should have strong doubts about the validity of the interpretations. (p. 8)

In the same manner that generalizability is achieved, researchers build and expand their corpus of exemplars from a variety of contexts and compare them against each other. The history of conversation analysis has been to collect and build a large corpus of conversations which demonstrate the repeated and coherent patterns of conversations (Heritage, 1984; Levinson, 1983).

The methodology of this project is different than traditional experimental research methodologies. However, as Hopper (1988) points out, "speech phenomena owe allegiance to no method" (p. 55). Hopper stresses the need for "both-and" thinking in order to "discern when an exemplar or an experiment may prove our best guide for a particular claim" (p. 61). Hopper ends his paper noting that "the exemplar and the experiment have much to teach each other: and teaching also involves learning" (p. 61).

This view fits well with Glaser and Strauss' (1967) position that qualitative research is not in opposition with quantitative research. Glaser and Strauss (1967), in their seminal work, state that "both forms of data are necessary" as quantitative is not used to test qualitative, but both are "used as supplements, as mutual verification" and "as different forms of data on the same subject, which, when combined, will generate theory" (p. 18).

Indeed, the ethnomethodological approach also fits well with aspects of intensive discovery-oriented process research (Greenberg, 1984, 1986a, 1986b; Greenberg & Pinsof, 1986; Gurman, Kniskern & Pinsof, 1986; Mahrer, 1988; Pinsof, 1986; Rice & Greenberg, 1984a, 1984b). While ethnomethodology and conversation analysis offer a different methodology than those of the researchers just listed, both approaches complement each other in their scientific validity. As Greenberg (1986b) states:

> The emphasis upon verification rather than discovery which is characteristic of contemporary psychotherapy research seems to be a distortion of the actual emphases in the practice of true science. Research in many of the physical sciences seems to devote much more time to seeking out possible regularities in phenomena than simply to proving that regularities they have noted are really there. . . . Science is an endeavour of trying to figure out what phenomena are about. (p. 711)

Ethnomethodology and conversation analysis strive for the same scientific goal. Ethnomethodology approaches are very intensive and rigorous approaches. As Henry David Thoreau stated, "No method nor discipline can supersede the necessity of being forever on the alert" (cited in Hopper, 1988, p. 61). Another relevant quote comes from Austin, who, in 1956, wrote:

> In the history of human inquiry, philosophy has the place of the central sun, seminal and tumultuous: from time to time it throws off some portion of itself to take station as a science, a planet, cool and well regulated, progressing steadily towards a distant final state. . . . Is it not possible that the next century may see the birth, through the joint labours of philosophers, grammarians, and numerous other students of language, of a true and comprehensive science of language? (cited in Levinson, 1983, p. 371)

KEY ISSUES TO BE ADDRESSED BY THIS STUDY

In order to discuss the two main purposes of this study, it is important to repeat that this methodology follows an inductive, discovery orientated approach. New knowledge is garnered through an intensive and rigorous analysis of the transcriptions and audiotape. The analysis is data-driven and avoids premature theory building. Therefore, specific hypotheses are not generated prior to the analytic procedures.

However, this study will address two key issues. First, the discourse of the therapy will be examined to better understand the therapeutic skills of William O'Hanlon. Through the analysis of the interactive conversation of the therapist and couple, various rhetorical devices used by all the participants will be explored. As Rogers (1942), many years ago, sought to find those "principles of change," this study will, in particular, explore the various rhetorical repertoires used by O'Hanlon.

How is change achieved? How does O'Hanlon develop the conversation towards a focus on solutions rather than problems? How does the participants' conversation create an organized pattern of meaning and action? This study will describe how patterns of change are constructed in the therapy session. While on the one hand it is specific to this one-session consultation by William O'Hanlon, the "how-to-do" analysis provided in this study can be valuable information for clinicians in all settings.

This leads to the second purpose of this study. This approach provides an alternate methodology (Hoshmand, 1989) for family therapy researchers and clinicians to consider the therapy context from a new perspective. Rather than studying the session through the theoretical lens of a particular school of family therapy, this approach considers how the participants themselves construct and define the meaning of their actions. This allows for a common language of change to be considered, regardless of the parent school of therapy.

This methodology is sensitive to the context as it avoids stripping events from their context in a reductionistic manner. It considers the sequential and reflexive interactions of both clients and therapist and it incorporates nonverbal and paralinguistic features into the analysis. It lays out the data for all to see, and thereby, leaves open the observer's biases. The analysis is sensitive to pattern and form, rather than focusing on substance.

In other words, this methodology is capable of following the cybernetic, systemic notions of family therapy. This complements the current research methodologies in offering an approach different and unique for filling in gaps in current family therapy research. To summarize, this project will provide the reader with how-to-do descriptive summaries of O'Hanlon's therapeutic work. In addition, a methodology, new to the family therapy field, is being introduced to complement current research strategies in the field.

PROCEDURES

Conversation analysis operates "using inductive search procedures" (Heritage, 1988, p. 131). The procedural steps used in this study were: (a) selection of a therapeutic conversation; (b) making an audio recording of the videotaped session; (c) transcribing the recording in some detail; (d) analysis. Hopper and Koch (1986) note that "analysis" is really the name of all four steps of this process as each step is reflexively related to each other in a circular manner of discovery.

The Therapeutic Session

The one-session consultation marital case of William O'Hanlon was selected for a variety of reasons. The case reflects the therapeutic approach of an important style of family therapy which combines Ericksonian strategies and brief therapy with a focus on solution-oriented behaviors. The consultation was viewed as a successful case by both the therapist and couple. In addition, all information regarding the case is recorded on the videotape, and thus, the entire therapeutic context is available for study.

William O'Hanlon is a respected therapist and author (O'Hanlon, 1987; O'Hanlon & Wilk, 1987; O'Hanlon & Weiner-Davis, 1989; O'Hanlon, 1989), both in family therapy and in Ericksonian therapy, which itself has direct links to family therapy theory and practice (Gale & Brown-Standridge, 1988). O'Hanlon has frequently presented at national conventions of the American Association of Marital and Family Therapy (AAMFT) and he was the outstanding presenter at the 1985 AAMFT national convention. He was also recently spotlighted in an interview in the *Family Therapy News* (Rawot, 1989).

O'Hanlon's therapeutic approach in the session used in this study follows his "solution-oriented" therapy (O'Hanlon & Weiner-Davis, 1989). Solution-oriented therapy can be traced to the work of Steve de Shazer (1982, 1985) and it is an emerging trend in therapy (Wynne, 1985). This approach to family therapy focuses on finding new behaviors that will be solutions to the presenting problem. The emphasis is that "solutions, not problems deserve our primary attention" in problem solving (Wynne, 1985, p. viii).

Solution-oriented therapy typically does "not find it useful to gather extensive historical information about the presenting problem" (O'Hanlon & Weiner-Davis, 1989, p. 38). Rather, the emphasis of solution-oriented therapy is toward generating new behaviors instead of considering reasons or explanations for understanding the clients' complaint.

It is a behavioral approach that is grounded in language. O'Hanlon and Weiner-Davis (1989) believe "that the creative and mindful use of language is perhaps the single most influential indirect method for creating contexts in which change is perceived to be inevitable" (p. 60). The therapeutic dialog endeavors to "channel the language" towards constructive solutions (p. 66).

This approach is different than the approach of cognitive psychology and fits well with the orientation of ethnomethodology. That is, language is seen as an interactive, constructive process as opposed to a system that represents what is "really" happening inside the person (Potter & Wetherell, 1987). O'Hanlon's therapeutic approach follows both a systemic orientation and relies on the active and performative nature of language. The contextual boundary of the therapy session (as recorded) provides all the relevant information necessary to understand the therapeutic process.

Therefore, the solution-oriented therapy of William O'Hanlon provides an excellent therapeutic approach in which to use conversation analysis to investigate the sequential and linguistic features of the therapeutic process. Through examining the therapy session conducted by William O'Hanlon, conversation analysis can reveal information important to both family therapy theory (in general) and to family therapy clinicians (of differing orientations).

The couple were seen by O'Hanlon in 1988 in a demonstration session observed by a group of professional therapists. The couple did agree to be videotaped at the time of therapy. The couple, both in their late twenties, had been married for eight years and had a two-year-old son. There had been problems in their marriage for the previous three years. During that time, both together and individually, they had seen various counselors and a psychiatrist. In the previous year the husband had been involved in an affair. The couple did separate for several months during this period, but at the time of the session, they were living together again.

The Audiorecording

The session was naturalistic for a family therapy session in that family therapy session are often videotaped and many times are even observed live by a team of professionals from the other side of a one-way mirror. A direct-feed audio recording was made from the videotape. The entire session lasted 45 minutes. The fidelity of sound was excellent and only minor, short segments were difficult to understand.

Transcription

Developing the transcripts involved multiple listening to the recorded session. A Norelco 2510 stenographic machine with foot pedal and ear phones was used to transcribe the recording. Approximately 80 hours were spent in repeated listening to the audiotape in order to create a detailed transcription. The transcription was done by the researcher as the process is more than simply putting words down on paper. As Potter and Wetherell (1987) state:

Transcription is a constructive and conventional activity. The transcriber is struggling to make clear decisions about what exactly is said, and then to represent those words in a conventional orthographic system. (p. 165)

Many others have also stressed the importance of the transcription process (Heritage, 1984, 1988; Hopper & Koch, 1986; Levinson, 1983; Sacks, 1987; Sacks, Schegloff, & Jefferson, 1974). Hopper and Koch (1986) point out that "new insights frequently emerge during the multiple listenings" and "the transcribing process almost inevitably finds interesting passages which can give projects their direction" (p. 12).

The process of transcribing the session is part of the discovery process. A slightly modified version of Jefferson's notational system (summarized in Schenkein, 1978) was used (see Appendix A). This notation included such details as: loudness of certain words; extended sounds; inhalations; exhalations; the timing with which speakers take turns, interrupt each other, or overlap each other's speaking; the timing of pauses.

While no transcribing method is complete, this type of transcription yields many paralinguistic features of the talk that are useful for microanalysis. The kinesic cues, or physical movements of the therapist and clients (head nods, major body gestures, shifting of positions), while recorded on the videotape, were minimally incorporated into the notations of the transcripts. At times the videotape was consulted in the analysis in order to amplify the analysis of the linguistic sequential organizational structure.

Analysis

Hopper and Koch (1986) report that the analysis stage is very difficult to describe. Potter and Wetherell (1987), for instance, describe part of the analysis process as "coding," but in a sense "quite different from standard techniques of content analysis" which codes "data into categories and look[s] at the frequency of occurrence" (p. 167). Heritage (1988) emphasizes that analysis is first discovering patterns of particular features of the talk and then finding deviant examples of those features. Hopper and Koch (1986) describe discovery as emerging "through pincers movements between *intuitive* judgements and *analytical* ones" (p. 16).

To understand these elements of analysis, Potter and Wetherell's (1987) approach will first be examined. Potter and Wetherell's (1987) use of "coding" entails collecting many instances of particular events, not to find results, "but to squeeze an unwieldy body of discourse into manageable chunks" (p. 167). The purpose of this stage of research is to produce a body of instances as inclusive as possible, rather than setting limits to that body.

For example, Buttny (1990) located various examples of blame account sequences within 18 pages of transcript of a couple therapy consultation.

Through this process of refining a large body of discourse into aworkable segment, Buttny selected a two-page episode that contained the features, for example, telling problems, blames, accounts and a therapeutic assessment of these points, that he was interested in analyzing.

Buttny (1990) included the transcript of this episode in the paper (so that the readers could assess his arguments and conclusions). Buttny then employed a microanalysis perspective to study the nonverbal aspects of blames and accounts. In this way Buttny was able to study the conjointly interacted negotiation between the therapist and clients regarding blame placing.

Pomerantz (1988) describes the analytic process as beginning with observations of the details of interactions. After considerable observation the analyst develops a proposal concerning an aspect of the social organization. This proposal attempts to account "how the details of the interaction came to be produced in the way they appear in the datum" (Pomerantz, 1988, p. 361). Following the formulation of a proposal, the analyst examines all relevant cases to see if the proposal needs to be modified in any manner.

In a similar fashion, Heritage (1988) describes analysis as first finding patterns of particular features within the body of the text. This is done through repeatedly listening to the recording and refining the transcription. Next, deviant examples of the pattern discovered earlier are sought. This means finding instances where those features of the talk are not first accepted.

An example of this can be observed in the basic conversational unit of adjacency pairs (Levinson, 1983). A question–answer is a type of adjacency pair where the predicted pattern is that a question will generate an answer. For example:

A: Are you ok?
B: I'm fine.

A deviant case would be finding an example where an initial question failed to elicit any response. When speaker A repeats the question again (or several more times), this indicates that the speaker is waiting for the patterned response of an answer. Such a deviant case follows:

A: Is there something bothering you or not?
   (1.0)
A: Yes or no
   (1.5)
A: Eh?
B: No.
   (Heritage, 1984, p. 248)

This deviant case thus verifies, for this instance, that the question–answer pattern is maintained. Speaker B does not answer speaker A at first, so speaker A continues two more times until an answer is provided. It can also be noted in the above example that the questioner repeated the question in increasingly truncated form, suggesting that the recipient did indeed hear the original question. Heritage (1988) states that "through deviant case analysis we can determine that account giving is not merely an empirically common feature that is associated with unexpected or unlooked for actions, but is a normatively required feature of such action" (p. 135).

As has been reported in the literature (Heritage, 1984; Hopper & Koch, 1986; Levinson, 1983; Pomerantz & Atkinson, 1984; Potter & Wetherell, 1987; Sacks, 1987; Schwartz & Jacobs, 1979; Sigman, Sullivan, & Wendell, 1986) there is no one set of procedures that conversation analysts or ethnomethodologists in general follow. Precisely because this research approach is grounded in a discovery mode, the procedures of research are intertwined. The stages of research "are not clear sequential steps, but phases which merge together in an order which may vary considerably" (Potter & Wetherell, 1987, p. 160).

An example of conversation analysis. A more detailed explanation of this type of analysis can be demonstrated through the following example. The transcription that follows is from session one of a three-session couple case in which the presenting problem was the wife's recurring incidences of paralysis. Medical doctors could find no cause for the paralysis. The therapist noted a similarity of the woman's paralysis with that of a state of a person experiencing deep trance. In this first session the therapist considered using hypnosis to help the woman "de-hypnotize" herself, but then shifted his approach and used a systemic reframe (in terms of viewing the problem as interactional) to resolve the presenting problem.

In seeking to understand why the therapist chose to work interactionally with the couple rather than simply with the wife, one segment in particular in the transcriptions highlights the interactional properties of the paralysis.

```
 1  W:  Well there once there was a little squabble
 2      between (.4) our daughters (.) They:::=
 3  H:  Quite a squabble.
 4  W:  Quite a squabble they ended up in court (.)
 5      over (.) ah (.) about some property and (.2)
 6      and some things and (.5) and I can't say
 7      that that had anything to do with it. It
 8      could hav:e
 9  H:  ((Clears throat)) It was stressful=
10  W:  =It was stressful because I couldn't take
11      neither side (.) of the family.
12  T:  When was this?
```

```
13  W:   This was:: = ((Turns to look at husband))
14  H:    = It's been 6 months I guess (.3) ((turns to
15         look at wife and nods)) uh hum.
16  W:   Uh hum.
17  T:   Is that squabble still happening?
18  H:   They they don't see each other (.3)
19         unless it is (.) ABSOLutely necessary
20         which they did (.hh) when she was in the
21         hospital they were in the same room at one
22         (.3) But (.) other than than that they
23         they (.3) don't want to be in each other's
24         presence.
```

In the analysis of this segment it is noted that in line 3 the husband (H) corrects and expands on the wife's (W) description of the squabble. The wife accepts his correction, and repeats the husband's words (line 4) and then amplifies her new understanding/description of the squabble (lines 4–7). The wife's repetition and amplification of the husband's correction, as seen in conversation analysis research, is typical of how a person repairs, or corrects what he/she has just said in order to express his/her new understanding (Heritage, 1984; Levinson, 1983; Potter & Wetherell, 1987).

In line 9 it appears that the husband is initiating a link between the daughters' squabble and the effect on his wife by noting "it was stressful." Lines 10 and 11 provide an analytical validation of this point. The wife accepts her husband's description immediately (as noted by the equal sign, which means no pause between turn taking). She also repeats what the husband had said in the prior turn and elaborates on why the daughters' squabble was so stressful. In her explanation of why it was stressful, further analytical validity is gained as she connects the stress to the children with the statement, "I couldn't take either side of the family." This statement is also viewed as an isomorphic analogy to her paralysis.

Further confirmation of the husband's interactional influence on the wife can be seen in lines 13 and 14. In line 13 the wife turns to her husband before answering, and elongates the word "was::" thus allowing time for the husband to answer the question. The husband answers "uh hum" (line 15) as he turns to look at the wife. The wife affirms this answer with "uh hum" on line 15.

Following the therapist's (T) question of "Is that squabble still happening?" (line 17), the husband proceeds to take the initiative (lines 18 to 24) to explain how the squabble connects to an earlier incidence of the wife's paralysis when she was hospitalized. This account further connects the paralysis to family interactional behaviors.

This example serves to highlight both the way in which accounts and explanations are sequentially and interpersonally constructed as well as the interpersonal influence that the husband had on the wife. While this is only one example from the three-session case, it is useful in highlighting the conversation analytic approach as an effective method for understanding the therapeutic process. In this example, conversation analysis helped in understanding the therapeutic decision to involve the family system in the therapeutic intervention.

SUMMARY

This study will incorporate the various elements of the ethnomethodological and conversation analytic approaches described above. The analysis of the conversation of the O'Hanlon therapy session will be presented in the following chapter. Particular patterns or features of the therapy talk will be pointed out through the use of exemplars. Deviant case examples will also be highlighted to strengthen the validity of the patterns found within the session.

Chapter 4
Analysis

This chapter will explicate William O'Hanlon's theoretical orientation and his therapeutic agenda and present various procedures which bind the interactive conversation of the clients into a solution-focused dialogue. First, several of the therapeutic interventions used in solution-oriented therapy, as described by O'Hanlon and Wilk (1987) and O'Hanlon and Weiner-Davis (1989) will be presented. Following this, a brief overview of the marital session under study will be provided. This annotated, sequential description of the session will use the protocols as described in the books by O'Hanlon and Wilk (1987) and O'Hanlon and Weiner-Davis (1989) to describe the therapeutic processes as they occurred in the session.

After viewing the session from the perspective of the therapist's agenda, the agendas of the wife and husband will be examined. Their agendas are inferred from the patterns of their talk and actions in the session. In analyzing how the husband's and wife's actions are "accountable" (Garfinkel, 1967), the documentation of the session will describe the procedures by which the clients produce their own behavior as well as understand and interact with the behavior of others. After this, the means by which the agendas of all three participants (therapist, wife, and husband) are woven together into an interactive conversation will be presented.

The procedures of "pursuing a response" will then be demonstrated to explain how O'Hanlon is able to continuously adjust his interventions to meet problematic responses from the wife or husband. As each person is pursuing a different agenda, it is crucial to examine how the therapist deals with these constantly shifting responses from the couple. These procedures of pursuing a response are the contextually sensitive moves that O'Hanlon incorporates to maintain the integrity of his therapeutic agenda. The nine procedures of pursuing a response will be explained and then demonstrated through extended exemplars from the session.

THE THERAPIST'S AGENDA

O'Hanlon's Theoretical Orientation

O'Hanlon clearly articulates his theoretical views in two books (O'Hanlon & Wilk, 1987; O'Hanlon & Weiner-Davis, 1989) and an unpublished

40

manuscript (O'Hanlon, 1989). Solution-oriented therapy is a pragmatic therapy that is concerned with the how of therapy rather than the why of therapy. Problems that clients bring into psychotherapy are viewed as perceptions, socially constructed by the client, as opposed to "real facts," such as a broken bone (O'Hanlon & Weiner-Davis, 1989, p. 52). The therapist is respectful of the clients' perceptions while helping them find or create goals and methods to resolve their presenting problems.

The goals of solution-oriented therapy are threefold. The first is to "change the 'doing' of the situation that is perceived as problematic." The second is to "change the 'viewing' of the situation that is perceived as problematic." The third is to "evoke resources, solutions and strengths to bring to the situation that is perceived as problematic" (O'Hanlon & Weiner-Davis, 1989, p. 126).

The key element common to these three aspects is the way in which clients "perceive" their situation, or in other words, what creates (causes) the problem and what resolves the problem. O'Hanlon (1989) stresses that until people distinguish problems in language, they are unable to perceive them as problems. Meaning and perception are a function of language, and therefore, language is the foundation of change. Reality is not a given, but rather, is shaped by the language we speak, the vocabulary we use, and the world view that we share is mirrored in these words (O'Hanlon & Weiner-Davis, 1989).

Language, according to this solution-oriented approach, is an interactive process where each of the above three goals are negotiated and defined through language transactions. Defining the problem, therefore, becomes a "purely verbal matter" (O'Hanlon & Wilk, 1987, p. 47). "The raw data of the client's (or clients') complaint" are "shaped by the therapeutic interaction" (O'Hanlon & Weiner-Davis, 1989, p. 54). Indeed, O'Hanlon and Wilk (1987) state that "the therapeutic problem to be worked on does not exist outside the therapist's office" as "it is a product of the client's and therapist's talking together" (p. 47).

The How-to-do Steps of Solution-oriented Therapy

O'Hanlon and Wilk (1987) state that ordinary language is the medium for therapeutic communication. They suggest that:

> A "fly on the wall" who did not know we were doing psychotherapy would not necessarily suspect that that was what we were doing: he would see and hear only an ordinary conversation. What defines the conversation as psychotherapy is simply our goal in conducting the conversation. (p. 177)

Yet, O'Hanlon and the other authors (O'Hanlon & Wilk, 1987; O'Hanlon & Weiner-Davis, 1989) also provide a wide variety of strategies for effec-

tively and specifically using language. Therapeutic conversations are delib-
erate and solution-oriented. Both books (O'Hanlon & Wilk, 1987; O'Hanlon
& Weiner-Davis, 1989) provide a variety of do's and don'ts for successfully
using this therapeutic approach. Emphasis is on changing the clients' descriptions, or view of their "problem." Rather than focusing on a history,
explanation, or cause for a problem, the therapist, from the beginning,
works towards changing the clients' perception of the problem.

This focus leads clients to describe solutions to their problems—in other
words, what has worked for them in the past, or what might work for them
in the future relative to solving their complaint. Exceptions to the problem,
or occasions when the problem was not present, are sought by the therapist
in order to develop a possible solution.

The five major steps in the therapy session include "joining," getting a
brief "description of the problem," "finding exceptions to the problem,"
"normalizing" and "goal-setting" (O'Hanlon & Weiner-Davis, 1989, pp. 75–
103). Within these steps, the therapist is continuously striving to alter the
description of the complaint from a problem focus towards a solution focus.

The therapist, from the very first meeting, negotiates the problem definition. The results of that negotiation will in turn influence the course of
the ensuing therapy. The nature of this negotiation is the construction of a
therapeutic reality and the (re)definition of the problem into a "presentable
problem—that is, one that doesn't have built-in barriers to its own solutions" (O'Hanlon & Wilk, 1987, p. 111). A problem without a workable
solution is likely to lead to an unsuccessful outcome.

While the therapist actively helps to redefine the problem, he/she works
from the goals that the client(s) describe. Goals are co-created through the
interaction between the vision of what the client(s) perceives is success and
what the therapist negotiates as achievable. The degree of success then
derives from the clients' reports such that "if clients say that what they
were complaining about is no longer a therapeutic issue or if what they are
complaining about is no longer happening, then therapy has succeeded"
(O'Hanlon & Wilk, 1987, p. 8).

In this process, the therapist takes an active role in directing the conversation towards goal-oriented solutions. A variety of strategies are used to
direct the conversation. O'Hanlon and Wilk (1987) describe their procedures as "working methods" which are not designed "as rigid procedures
and rules, but as guidelines for therapists" (p. 110). Indeed, they view their
"working methods" simply as signposts that will become obsolete as better
descriptions are developed.

In examining these working procedures, 10 strategies were selected
based on the criteria of using interventions employed in one-session cases
and that are not derivitive of another intervention. These interventions
were collected from both O'Hanlon and Wilk's (1987) book and O'Hanlon

and Weiner-Davis' (1989) book. These 10 interventions will be discussed below.

1. "Speaking the client's language" is a strategy of joining in which the therapist selectively uses the client's preferred terminology, metaphors, and emotional tone. This can include using the same words, phrases, or metaphors that the client uses as well as using the same paralanguage. This strategy helps to both convince the client that he/she is understood and direct the client's talk towards specific directions.

2. "Presupposing change" involves posing questions that are designed such that they imply that change is forthcoming. Either by selecting a specific verb tense, or implying the occurrence of a particular event, the client is led to believe that a solution will be achieved. For example, the use of past tense, "How much *did* you used to smoke?" implies that the cigarette smoking is no longer occurring. This is different than asking, "How much do you smoke a day?" which implies that the smoking behavior is still occurring (O'Hanlon & Wilk, 1987, p. 125). Presuppositional questions are designed to be open-ended, leaving open the possibility of change. "What good things happened?" implies there were in fact good things to be noticed, which is different than asking, "Were there any good things that happened?"

3. "Multiple-choice questions" are questions asked that offer possible answers. This serves to not only save "time by making clear to the client the sort of information we are looking for, but gently steers the client in the direction we are wanting to go" (O'Hanlon & Wilk, 1987, p. 120).

4. "Therapeutic interruption" occurs when the therapist, at key times, interrupts the client in order to divert the conversation towards another direction. The therapist will interrupt either to clarify his/her understanding of the clients' position, or to preempt the clients from "verbally paint-[ing] themselves into an unhelpful corner" (O'Hanlon & Wilk, 1987, p. 120).

5. "Normalizing the problem" is a strategy which is designed to help the client view his/her "problem" not as a pathology but as an everyday phenomenon. Through telling a story or anecdote, or describing other clients (or sharing a personal experience), the therapist provides examples of other people facing similar problems. Through elaborating the solutions employed by the people in these stories the clients are encouraged to perceive their difficulty in a new light.

6. "Summarizing with a twist" is the strategy whereby the therapist summarizes significant elements of the preceding section of talk, but in addition, will introduce a slight change in description. The twist is designed to steer an aspect of the summation towards a solution-oriented perspective. Once the client accepts this version of the summary, the therapist then proceeds to use it as the new baseline of the client's summary.

7. "Utilization" involves accepting whatever the client offers in the session. Rather than rejecting, disagreeing, or resisting the client's views or behaviors, the therapist incorporates (utilizes) the client's view or behavior into a useful perspective. The utilization approach involves "building a bridge from where the client is now to the eventual goal" (O'Hanlon & Wilk, 1987, p. 133).

8. "Providing obvious solutions" is the strategy which offers direct advice. This strategy has the therapist offering common-sense suggestions. The therapist may suggest new behaviors or new ways of interacting. In couple therapy, specific descriptions of clients' goals are sought and often negotiated in a very direct, quid pro quo manner.

9. "Introducing doubt" is the strategy that challenges the clients' rigid beliefs about the problem. Helping the clients to be specific, finding exceptions to their beliefs, channeling their language from negative labels towards action descriptions and telling stories of others who succeeded at a similar problem will serve to change the clients' views. When the client doubts the rigid nature of his/her own problem, he/she is more likely to consider a solution.

10. "Future focus" is the strategy of setting specific and concrete goals towards which the clients are to work. Through directing the conversation towards future success while anticipating possible obstructions to success, the clients are led to focus on future success rather than present problems.

The above is only a partial listing of structured strategies suggested by the authors. As O'Hanlon and Wilk (1987) state, these procedures "provide far from an adequate description of what we do in therapy. We are continually seeking further and updated descriptive generalizations for identifying what it is we do that seems effective" (p. 111). This list does, however, provide an organizing schema from which to begin analyzing the marital session.

A Cursory Analysis of the Session from the Perspective of the Therapist's Agenda

From the very beginning of the consultation O'Hanlon sets the stage for the conversation to proceed in a particular direction. He states that:

```
05   . . . I've I specifically asked (.hhh) not
06   to know anything about what >your situa-
07   tion is so I can< come with a fresh vie::w
08   and (.hhh) giveye some fresh ideas hope-
09   fully (.) and >help you move along to where
10   where ever you want to go: (.hhh)< . . .
13                            . . . . maybe to
```

14   help me orient to where we are suppos::ed
15   to go where you hope to go (.hhh) ho:w
16   will you know ((swallowed)) if we've done
17   wonderful things here ((wife nods yes)) and
18   everything is worked out . . .

In this manner O'Hanlon is describing how he wants the conversation to proceed. He is emphasizing a discussion geared towards future goals (and not problems) that can be clearly described.

The wife answers the therapist's questions, however, beginning with a short history of their eight years of marriage and their current difficulties (lines 42–78). She describes the first three years as happy. She does state that when they set goals they have an easier time succeeding and working together. Following her statement that right now "our most important thing is communication" (lines 80–81) she immediately shifts to saying "and that's what led up to this point recently" (lines 85–86) as she notes the date on which she found out about her husband's affair.

In the past eight months, since finding out about the affair, she describes how difficult a time it has been for her. She moved in with her mother and sister to have someone help with child care, but that was stressful too. She saw a psychiatrist, but that did not help as she says, "I needed someone to shake me and be alive again" (lines 184–185). The wife sums up her position with the statement:

197   I think um (.5) there was a lot of lies a
198   lot of lot of just hateful things that
199   were done (.hhh) ((therapist nods yes))
200   and he kinda pleads temporary insanity
201   which I think is a very poor excuse
202   ((therapist nods yes and no)) and I find
203   that hard to forgive him for that and =

The therapist follows the wife's summation by asking the husband about the affair, "is it done?" (line 215). This move by O'Hanlon appears to serve three purposes. It is the therapist's first attempt to involve the husband in the conversation. It will get the information that the affair is over and that the problem is in the past. An answer of yes will also allow the conversation to move toward developing solution-oriented behavior to help the relationship between the husband and wife.

The husband responds with "I want it to be done, yes" (line 220). This answer implies that the affair may not be totally finished and, therefore, does not give O'Hanlon a clear statement from which to pursue a solution-focused conversation. O'Hanlon, then repeats the question, and using the multiple choice question intervention, offers a possible answer (emphasizing the word *past*) for the husband by posing, "Ok, I mean is the contact with this person in the <u>past</u> or is that still going on?" (lines 222–224). The husband answers by saying that it is 95 percent over as the girlfriend still tries to contact him.

O'Hanlon accepts this answer but he also adds to it (summarizing with a twist) by crediting the husband with actively shoving it aside.

```
233   she still sometimes tries to ahm get some
234   contact with ((husband nods yes)) you as
235   much as possible you (.8) (.hh) you've
236   been shoving it to the side.
```

As the wife adds that "she's [the girlfriend] called me whenever she" (line 238) the therapist interrupts the wife before she finishes her statement. This seems to be a maneuver (therapeutic interruption) to avoid the wife's possible focus on the problem, that is, the girlfriend, and to shift the conversation towards resolving the problem. O'Hanlon continues his turn by summing up the session to that point but with a twist:

```
246   but for the most part (.) th (.hh) I
247   assume the reason you two are here
248   together is you're saying ok: if it's pos-
249   sible to put this thing back together (.)
250   to get ((wife nods yes)) (.) to some good
251   place ((husband nods yes)) that's what we
252   would like to do we would like to (.hh)
253   get the affair behind us and get back
254   ((wife nods yes)) to:: (.hh) some of
255   things that we used to do ((husband nods
256   yes)) that were good like the first three
257   years as you said that were happier,
258   closer, less conflict (.hh) and be able to
259   lea::ve this one behind and say how can I
260   (.) somehow let go of this ((wife nods
261   yes)) and work through it ((husband nods
262   yes)) or forgive (.) or forget or (.hh) if
263   not forgive and forget somehow put this
264   (.hh) in its place so that we can: move on
265   and build something else . . .
```

This summary presupposes that since the couple came for the session, they must want to get the affair behind them and put their marriage back together (future focus). The therapist asks a multiple-choice question of the wife, whether she would prefer to: leave the affair behind; let go of the affair; forgive the husband; forget the affair; or put the affair in its place.

Each one of these choices presuppose ending the problem and moving towards a solution, that is, to "build something else."

O'Hanlon then presents a figurative comparison of skating or getting off the ice (lines 268–273) as another way of prodding them to work towards resolution in their relationship. He then presupposes what the husband may be thinking. He suggests that the husband would like to say "I don't want to hear it anymore" and "I think I paid my dues::" (lines 282–283). O'Hanlon then suggests that the husband would want to state " I admit: >I was wrong and it was crazy and all this stuff<" (lines 285–286). This suggested paraphrase attributes to the husband that he both admits responsibility and states that the affair is over.

O'Hanlon then takes the next 11 lines (lines 292–303) to slowly build up to the question of when were there times "that actually things: went *ok . . ." (lines 303–304). This slow buildup to the question is an Ericksonian strategy that creates a sense of curiosity for the clients in order to increase the importance of the question (Erickson, 1980). This move also is the solution-oriented approach of leading the conversation toward a discussion about solutions. The therapist offers a variety of possible answers after asking this question (lines 304–317).

The husband immediately responds with an answer to the therapist's query. He states that a good time he and his wife had together, in the midst of the difficulties, was a day trip to a game park in New York. The wife, however, disagrees with the husband's assessment. She states that the day trip to the park was not a good time "because I knew she [girlfriend] was still there" (line 328). The wife then adds her doubt about the husband's commitment to their relationship (lines 331–345). The therapist listens to the wife, occasionally acknowledging her views, until finally he interrupts her:

364   . . . [right, ok] ((husband
365   shrugs shoulders)) So::, so but (.) that's
366   the ki::nd of thing you w::ould like to do
367   in the future you know like sp sp spend
368   like you just went ah where did go over
369   to, New York?

This interruption ignores what the wife had just said about her concerns, and instead, returns back to the topic of the day trip to New York. This is a maneuver to find out if the day trip was a possible solution activity.

The wife does respond (at least minimally) to O'Hanlon's question with "New York, yeah" (line 370). O'Hanlon therefore continues by asking for additional times that were perceived as good. The wife, however, returns to discussing her lack of communication with her husband as well as her mistrust and hatred for him. This leaves O'Hanlon confused as he asks:

415   [((therapist crosses legs, similar to
416   wife's posture)) Right (.1) and so, and
417   so what, I'm a little mystified given that
418   (.hhh) (.4) lately you've been communicat-
419   ing more, and (ah:?)=

The wife answers that they just recently moved back together. O'Hanlon responds with the use of humor by challenging the wife, "NOBODY COULD GET ME TO MAKE THAT DECISION *WHY*:::? was I so:: crazy?" (lines 432–433). The use of humor here is likely the therapist's maneuver to get the wife to challenge or doubt her rigidly held belief that nothing will make her forgive her husband or work towards resolution with him (O'Hanlon & Wilk, 1987, pp. 174–177). In addition, this question is another way to find solution-oriented behaviors that the couple may have already employed.

The wife replies that the girlfriend calling her on a daily basis was proof that her husband was not contacting the girlfriend anymore. The wife then added:

468   [yeah,
469   yeah ((unfolds arms)) and so so ah she
470   said "he called me and said he wouldn't
471   have anything to do with me and that it
472   was over with between us." And so I knew
473   this and obviously he had proven to me
474   (.hhh) that finally he was possibly gonna
475   drop her.=

The therapist sums up the wife's statement by stating "=so you saw some action from him and that's what you needed to see? ((wife nods yes))" (lines 476–477). This adds the twist of implying and attributing a definite action by the husband to terminate the affair. O'Hanlon then adds:

483   . . . he doesn't want that and he's ((wife
484   nods yes)) ge getting that (1.3) tossing
485   that away ehh you know avoiding that (.hh)
486   and saying *OK* I Would like this and then
487   you had to really say "(.hhh) alright I
488   seen some action now:: can:: (.) I: (.)
489   possibly:: (.2) (.hh) think about: getting
490   back together" And you and at that point
491   you said "OK (.1) I'm willing to try"
492   ((wife nods yes)) (1.0) Ok, so you two
493   moved back together and now you just had
494   this trip to New York, yes=

The therapist, in the above maneuver, is returning to the trip to New York as an example of solution-oriented behavior. The wife, however, challenges the therapist's summary by saying, "I don't think I really wanted to move back together" (lines 496–498). She then adds that other factors, such as financial problems, problems with her own family of origin, difficulty in finding a home, and stress all contributed to her returning to live with her husband.

O'Hanlon responds to her concerns with the utilization approach (O'Hanlon & Wilk, pp. 132–134). He states, "I think that's important to include that in there" (lines 583–584) in order to help them move on and develop:

```
604          . . .common goals and going
605    for it, (.hh) and we've gotta inclu::de
606    (.) ((points to the husband)) the hurt and
607    the upset (*>in the past<*) the doubts
608    that you have in the present and that you
609    might have in the future (.hh) and some of
610    the >hurt that you might have in the
611    future< ((wife nods yes)) let's: include
612    that because if we leave it out it's gonna
613    come back and bonk us on the head . . .
```

In this manner, the therapist is building a bridge from the problem perspective to the solution perspective, incorporating the wife's doubts. This is an attempt to ratify or accept her concerns, and then utilize these same concerns as the means for change in a positive direction.

To further push this point, O'Hanlon follows with a story regarding other couples that he has worked with (O'Hanlon & Wilk, 1987, pp. 140–144). His story is isomorphic to the couple's situation in that the scenario of the story mirrors the solution-oriented approach that he is employing with the couple. The characters in the story are a couple experiencing conflicts and an affair and are facing the decision of continuing the relationship or not. The purpose of this story, like his earlier comments, is to utilize the doubts and concerns of the wife to help rebuild a positive relationship. As O'Hanlon relates the tale, he begins to talk directly to the couple (line 630), and it is unclear whether the therapist is telling a story or offering direct advice:

```
618    Sometimes when I see couples and things
619    have happened, whatever it may be lots of
620    conflicts or affairs or whatever it may be
621    (.hhh) that (.) it's: the way I think
622    about it is sometimes when you first got
623    married when you first fell in love or
624    whatever, it's like this ((said slowly))
```

625 *golden light just sorta shinn:ed all
626 over you * ((wife nods yes)) and you felt
627 (.hhh) you know ah lov:ing and goo::d
628 ((wife nods yes)) an:d clo:se to each
629 other and >all this stuff . . .

As it becomes clearer that he is talking directly to the husband and wife and not simply telling a tale of another couple, O'Hanlon asks the wife:

676   . . . when you finally wash away
677 the problems and deal with those and move
678 on: (1.0) (.hh) then: you gotta see, is
679 there anything left in terms of of your
680 feelings? ((wife nods yes)) But for now:
681 I'd say have your doubts . . .
      . . . .
696   . . . Include those
697 doubts and also be able to listen to em.
698 Say, ((looks at husband)) and and don't
699 take it personally, it's like >if you
700 doubt our relationship then we don't have
701 a future< ((wife nods yes)) *No:* (.hhh)
702 (.4) you can doubt our relationship and we
703 may still have a future ((wife nods yes))
704 if we could include those doubts.

In these two segments, O'Hanlon is implying that the problem will come to an end, the question is just "when." He also is implying that having those doubts does not mean that the relationship cannot be saved. In addition, he is advising the wife to make the decision for herself regarding her feelings for her husband and whether she is willing to pursue healing the relationship.

In this turn sequence (lines 696–704), O'Hanlon is also utilizing the doubt of both the wife and the husband. He is likely doing this because the wife has already demonstrated that she will not easily let go of her concerns. Therefore, he is utilizing the concerns to lead her in a new direction. The therapist also suggests to the husband that he accept the wife's doubts without trying to "pressure her too much" (lines 715–716). The husband responds to this by recalling another exception to their problem. The husband mentions that they had been trying to talk to each other every day at a special time (lines 720–721). The wife agrees that this does work and it is helpful (line 729).

However, as the wife continues to talk, her comments return to the girlfriend and concerns for the marriage. The wife does say "I promised myself I just said today I am not gonna bring her up" (lines 758–760), so that she can have at least one day without her (the girlfriend) being discussed. The therapist labels this as the wife's "vow: to take one day vacation from the thoughts about her" (lines 777–779) as he asks if this is an effective solution. The wife reports that it is effective. She then adds that on the car ride to the consultation she and her husband had had a good conversation.

As the wife relates the good communication she had with her husband in the car that day (lines 786–788), the therapist introduces another story (line 810). This story is of other people he has seen, who, in situations similar to the husband and wife, were dealing with communication and relationship problems. Through the telling of the story O'Hanlon is stressing the importance of the husband and wife spending time together communicating. Telling this story allows the therapist the opportunity to normalize and encourage their solution-oriented behaviors (O'Hanlon & Wilk, 1987, pp. 121–123; O'Hanlon & Weiner-Davis, 1989, pp. 93–100).

O'Hanlon, after stressing the importance of this type of solution behavior (time together communicating), then suggests a counseling technique (lines 834–871). In describing this technique of listening and repeating back what you heard from the other person, the therapist is teaching them a common sense solution, he is normalizing the wife's feelings, and he is encouraging the husband to accept her feelings. In addition, O'Hanlon is also suggesting new ways for them to view their emotional interactions (as a method to resolve issues).

O'Hanlon then uses humor to challenge the wife's views of the girlfriend (O'Hanlon & Wilk, 1987, pp. 174–177; O'Hanlon & Weiner-Davis, 1989, pp. 137–138):

```
876   T:   like if he all the sudden had the thought
877        (.hh) you know, I thought about her
878        today, (.HHH) NRRR ((wife nods yes)) you
879        know push your button you go ballistic =
880   W:   (laughter)
881   T:   = you know off you go (.hh) ((husband
882        smiles)) and say OK, in instead, sometime
883        in the future just be able to hear him say
884        say (.hh) he had this random thought, ((wife
885        nods yes)) it didn't mean he's gonna go
886        bac::k with with her it didn't mean he
887        doesn't lov:e you, it didn't mean he's not
888        committed here (.hhh) but just that occa-
889        sionally he has this thought. =
```

This humor serves to challenge the wife's rigid notions that any thoughts regarding the girlfriend mean a problem. The therapist adds a future component to this in helping the wife to anticipate that while the girlfriend may come up in conversation, it need not mean there is a problem. It can also be noted that in this segment the therapist is using verb tense changes to tie future change into the present (O'Hanlon & Wilk, 1987, p. 125).

The wife, however, responds to these suggestions by stating:

```
897                        [(You
898   know) that was one of our I think one of
899   our big things though that led to a lot of
900   this (.hh) is: that he wasn't telling me
901   how he feel:s=
```

As the wife continues her comments her anger begins to build and her focus shifts back to problems rather than resolution (lines 903–912). Much of her anger is directed at the husband for not expressing his feelings. When the husband responds, "I'm usually the last: to know how I feel" (lines 924–925) the therapist uses humor to return he conversation back to a solution focus:

```
926   ((laughter)) (yea:h right) ((slaps knee))
927   It's like, "huh:: I won::der ho:w ((wife
928   laughs)) I do: fee:l? ah::? goo::d ques-
929   tion::" an:d so:: ah so during those con-
930   versations though that you've had, those
931   you know sitting down every night (.hh)
932   have you been able to get a little more to
933   that?
```

In this segment the therapist exaggerates the husband's statement. In addition, the therapist is introducing the idea that these nightly meetings may be helping the husband to better express his feelings.

The husband responds by saying:

```
941   I need some kind of an exercise or some-
942   thing that would ((therapist nods yes))
943   (.6) help me (1.2) do that,
```

The husband mentions that he does much better when he writes (lines 945–947), so O'Hanlon suggests that he keep a journal. The therapist presents this task with humor as he comments:

```
959   you may notice ((wife nods yes)) (.hhh)
960   that under the pressure of ((leans toward
961   husband)) >what are you feeling what are
962   you feeling what are you feeling< (.hh) I
```

963   mean probably what I would say is, <u>Pres-</u>
964   <u>sure!</u> ((laughs))

Both the husband and wife laugh at this. This statement also models for the husband what he might be feeling, and how to express his feelings. O'Hanlon then begins another story of other couples that he has worked with (line 994). This story, like the other stories told in the session, are isomorphic to the couple's situation. It serves the purpose of elaborating the task assignment, normalizing the solution behaviors and encouraging them to do the writing exercise (O'Hanlon & Wilk, 1987, pp. 121–123 and 140–145).

The wife agrees with this assignment by commenting that indeed, "we kinda, we kinda did that" (lines 1019–1020). With the couple agreeing to this solution-oriented behavior, O'Hanlon, playing "devil's advocate" (line 1064), directs them towards a future scenario where a problem might occur again. This serves to help the couple devise their own solution-oriented behaviors. The wife answers, "to make a (.2) daily scheduled time" (line 1077). The therapist highlights his response to her:

1080   [(((therapist pounds fist onto
1081   his hand)) <u>To actually make an appoint-</u>
1082   <u>ment]</u> with each other and keep that
1083   <u>appointment</u> ((wife nods yes and unfolds
1084   her arms)) come hell or high water

As the couple discuss the difficulty in scheduling time together, the therapist offers a story of himself and his wife describing how they schedule time together (lines 1189–1221). This story serves the purpose of offering new solution-oriented behaviors, while normalizing their current behaviors. This is especially apparent when O'Hanlon states that when he and his wife do not keep their commitment to each other, "cause if we <u>don't</u> >we find that we don't<" (lines 1217–1218), nothing serious happens.

O'Hanlon then suggests to the wife:

1233   . . . First of all I
1234   don't think you should trust him until
1235   you're really sure he's trustworthy, so
1236   (.) <u>that</u> somewhat takes time I mean when
1237   you said "Well: now I've got some evidence
1238   from <u>her</u> ((wife nods yes)) calling me up
1239   (.hhh) (.hhh) and now from him directly
1240   (.hh) that he's not pursuing that <u>as far</u>
1241   <u>as I can tell.</u> ((wife nods yes)) I mean
1242   you can't follow him around 24 hours a day

```
1243   >but as far as you can tell he's not pur-
1244   suing that< (.hhh) Now as you get more
1245   time under your belt maybe you'll feel
1246   more secur:e, that he's not pursuing that
1247   and he's reall::y trul::y ((wife nods
1248   yes)) given it up left it (.) behind.
```

The therapist is utilizing the wife's feelings at this juncture by accepting her doubts. He reminds her of the evidence she has already of the girlfriend calling her and of the husband's commitment to her. O'Hanlon also reminds her that it will take time till she can trust him. In this manner he is embedding the notion that the husband has changed, and that she will see these changes over time and in the future.

O'Hanlon then suggests a ceremony that the couple can do together to further facilitate a healing of their relationship (lines 1257–1259). He presents this ceremony as something that he has had other couples do (thus normalizing the task). As he builds up the ceremony through an extended delivery, O'Hanlon also challenges the wife to consider whether she is indeed ready to renew "their marriage vows" (line 1270).

This raises a concern for the wife as she recalls how her husband is "in a hurry to put his wedding band on" (lines 1279–1282). O'Hanlon, rather than disagreeing with her, accepts her concerns and utilizes them into the ceremony "That maybe part of the ceremony (.1) This is good." (lines 1287–1288). He then tells the wife, "good, so don't put em on before you're ready" (lines 1301–1302). O'Hanlon then offers multiple-choice questions to help her identify how she will know when she is ready and he uses humor to help her change her perspective on the ring exchanging ceremony.

```
1303   HOW:: will you know you're ready? Will it
1304   be fee::ling will it be some more tim::e
1305   (.hh) will it be something else that needs
1306   to happen so that that I that I actually
1307   think (.hh) if you could possibly arrange
1308   it would be part of the ceremony, is the
1309   exchanging of rings again ((husband and
1310   wife both nod yes)) (1.0) But really
1311   having the other person put it on with
1312   your permission not like (.) here ((wife
1313   nods yes)) (.hh) I'm gonna jam this on
1314   your finger cause I think it needs that=
```

The wife, however, continues to express a great deal of concern regarding letting go of the husband's ex-girlfriend, and she states that "still I get angry because he pleads temporary insanity with the the hurt that he had done me" (lines 1382–1384). The therapist responds with another multiple-choice question suggesting to the wife various ways she can know to trust her husband and do a remarriage ceremony.

```
1395   the question is (.) what would it take to
1396   be ready to (.2) *put that ring on again?*
1397   (2.0) Will it tak:e (1.0) more communica-
1398   tion? (.1) will it take more time? (.8)
1399   How:: can (.) he sho:w you (.2) tha:t (.)
1400   he's really committed this >time? is<
1401   there a way that you can think of that he
1402   can show you or again will it be time?
1403   (.hhh)
```

Each of these choices imply that there is indeed a method that can be used to demonstrate that the husband has changed. In this segment O'Hanlon is using many pauses to further highlight the significance of his observation.

The wife answers "I think it's gonna be time" (line 1404), but then she again returns to her fears and concerns about what her husband had done to her (lines 1425–1427). She recalls that her husband told her to call anytime to check up on him, and she wonders why her husband wants her to check up on him.

```
1432   =(.hh) I'm like does he want me to check up
1433   on him because he (.) doesn't (.) trust
1434   himself or does he want me to check up on
1435   him to make me feel better? . . .
```

O'Hanlon suggests that she ask the husband for his answer. The husband responds that "I want you to check up on me so you'll feel better?" (lines 1442–1443). O'Hanlon accepts this answer and then embeds it into a story of a task that he assigns to other couples to help them establish trust (lines 1445–1450). The therapist then gives an analogy of an elevator failing.

```
1483                      . . . everything
1484   went fine you got in the elevator one time
1485   and the cable snapped and you fell down
1486   ((wife nods yes)) (.hhh) and you survived
1487   (.8) mean: (.) if you actually had to ride
1488   an elevator again or decided you know I
1489   need to overcome this this fear (.) how:
1490   many times would it take for you to ride
1491   the elevator ((wife nods yes)) before you
1492   trusted it again . . .
```

The analogy is representative of their current dilemma and poses for the wife the only way of knowing for sure if she can trust her husband is to take a risk.

The therapist next acknowledges the wife's feelings, her doubts and pains, and tells her not to put that ring back on until she is ready (lines 1415–1416). In this way O'Hanlon is joining the wife by accepting her concerns and encouraging her not to force herself to change. This maneuver seems to be a way to work with the wife's actions. Rather than trying to come up with a solution-oriented approach that the wife has repeatedly rejected by turning back to her doubts, O'Hanlon preempts her rejection by encouraging her to keep the doubts and concerns. This serves to both avoid her possible rejections as well as normalize her behaviors.

O'Hanlon then offers some more suggestions through another story of another couple. This story is isomorphic to the couple's situation as it describes a married couple dealing with the wife's affair. In his story, O'Hanlon describes a ritual of letting go and burying a symbol of the affair (lines 1453–1461). He then suggests to the couple in the consultation, that they find a symbol that they can "burn: or bury or (.hhh) throw off the pier" (line 1466).

The wife at first cannot think of anything concrete that she can use as a symbol. After some discussion she does recall having a bill for $48.00 for roses that her husband had bought the girlfriend, and says "we can burn that" (line 1526). The therapist immediately supports this behavior. The wife comments with a humorous side note that "I had a baby to get a dozen roses I don't know what she did to get a dozen roses" (lines 1531–1533). Both the wife and therapist laugh at the humor of this view.

O'Hanlon then jokes about how the wife would make a good detective. The wife laughs at this. She then describes how she wanted to wash the girlfriend away. This likely represents a good sign that the wife is accepting the idea of letting go of the problem (affair) and thinking of possible solutions. O'Hanlon follows up on her idea of washing her (the girlfriend) away by telling of a ceremony that he has suggested to other clients (lines 1671–1684). He describes a ritual of taking a bath together. As O'Hanlon presents this ritual, he reviews many of the earlier themes from the session, that is, letting go of the doubts, willingness to forgive, letting go of the anger.

In this sequence, O'Hanlon embeds multiple-choice questions with answers.

```
1721          . . . How can you find a way:: to
1722   really declare (.2) this (.) I I'm ready
1723   to let this one go or wash ((wife nods
1724   yes)) this one away or I intend to wash
```

```
1725   this away (1.0) ((therapist looks at hus-
1726   band and then the husband nods yes)) so
1727   moving back together is: sort of a ritual
1728   (.) and going through the step ((wife nods
1729   yes)) and (.hhh) gedding rid of whatever
1730   is another ritual (.hhh) gedding rid of
1731   of the cigarettes out of the car is another
1732   ritual that's a way ((wife nods yes)) to
1733   sort of declare (.hhh) ok that was our
1734   life then: (.hh) and we can (.) and now
1735   we: want to set our sights on the future
1736   and on our goals:
```

O'Hanlon in this segment is implying that changes have already occurred in the relationship. Another summary is then provided by the therapist as he comments:

```
1741                           . . . that
1742   doesn't mean we can't have some of the
1743   doubts and fears:: and (.hhh) and all
1744   that: (.1) but (.1) we're to going to
1745   declare that we're in this together and
1746   we're going for ((wife nods yes)) it (.hh)
1747   (1.3) and any moment (.2) you could
1748   bail out or you could bail out that always
1749   a possibility but at least you declare
1750   here's our intention to go (1.0) towards
1751   getting back together (1.1) . . .
```

This segment lets the wife know she always has the option to "bail out" of the relationship, but implies that perhaps she and her husband's intentions are really toward getting back together (lines 1747–1751). O'Hanlon then asks the couple if there is anything else they want to talk about before they finish.

The wife answers by first saying no, and then expressing some of her concerns again. The therapist then encourages her to check up on her husband any time if that helps her to feel better.

```
1771  W:  ((husband looks towards wife as if for her
1772       to answer)) *I I don't know* (2.1) *I
1773       think I gotten pretty much what I want out
1774       ((therapist nods yes and husband nods
1775       yes)) and I don't know*
1776  T:  *OK* (.hhh)=
1777  W:  Then I asked him and that's what bothers me
```

```
1778        most ((folds arms over chest)) is just the
1779        trust in him (.hhh)=
1780  T:    =yeah right ((nodding yes, coughs))=
1781  W:    =how to build that back that's what I have
1782            to do before I can do anything I I feel
1783            that's important like before I can go any-
1784            where ((unfolds her arms from chest))
1785            (.hhh) is to get that trust back
1786  T:    right and and you know as much as you
1787        doubted maybe his motives I think that
1788        what he offered is (.hh) is what is an
1789        essential key (.2) to be able to check up
1790        on him any time you may ((wife nods yes))
1791        think "AWWW I shouldn't be so paranoid I
1792        shouldn't have to check up ((wife nods
1793        yes)) (on him) does he think he is not
1794        trustworthy" (.hhh) I think his statement
1795        was "I'm trustworthy now I want you to
1796        kno::w I'm trustworthy ((wife nods yes))
1797        to really find it out and if you need to
1798        check up on me that's what you need to do=
```

The wife responds to O'Hanlon's comments by noting that she tends to always look at the negative side of things.

```
1816   There is a kinda negative side to things
1817   like (.1) this you know I always (.hh)
1818   pull from the negative I know I never look
1819   at anything positive you know I say well
1820   he's not saying this for me to check up on
1821   him he's saying this because he he doesn't
1822   trust himself I always look at things that
```

The therapist accepts this position, but adds to it a positive twist that, in fact, she "looks at both sides of it" (lines 1730–1731). O'Hanlon does state that perhaps "you DWELL: a liddle more on the negative" (lines 1731–1732), but she should include that in their relationship. He normalizes her negativity by stating:

```
1846             . . . . and you better
1847   be able to include the the down sides of
1848   the pressures of being married and (.hhh)
1849   having financial difficulties or having a
1850   kid or whatever it may be (.hhh) or it's
1851   not for you (.1) you know marriage isn't
1852   for you (.) obviously . . .
```

This statement presents the wife's doubts and concerns as normal to many situations, and therefore, having doubts does not mean that the husband is having an affair. O'Hanlon then continues by commenting that affairs typically do not last. He implies that the husband wants a stable relationship that will last a long time with someone "who has the kind of qualities that you have" (lines 1869–1870) and who is the mother of their child. O'Hanlon concludes this segment by commenting:

```
1874        . . . you've tentatively sort
1875    of said I'll think ((wife nods yes))
1876    about making this decision and (.hhh)
1877    your: actions seem to support that now
1878    you'll see see whether ultimately this is
1879    the *kinda marriage you want to have*
1880    (.1) (.hh) or you want to be married.
1881    ((husband nods yes))
```

This summary implies that they are already on the road of checking out solution-oriented behaviors in their life.

The wife, however, responds with expressing still more of her concerns about the instability of the relationship. Again, O'Hanlon responds with encouraging her to keep those doubts. He then uses humor to exaggerate her situation.

```
1929        . . . even if you think ((in sing-
1930    song voice)) "Oh I should be done with this
1931    no:w I shouldn't be thinking ((wife nods
1932    yes)) about this I shouldn't be saying
1933    this DADADADAD" >even if you think< oh I
1934    wish she'd get through this (.hhh)
```

The wife laughs at this exaggeration and admits that she does bring the girlfriend up too often. O'Hanlon reminds her of her vow to take a vacation from thinking of the ex-girlfriend just for a short time. He then suggests that she extend the vacation to longer periods till she is ready to let go of it all together (lines 1965–1969). This implies that the doubts will indeed come to a finish. O'Hanlon also adds that they will find a new norm in their marriage.

The wife responds that she wants the old norm back, while the husband wants "a new and improved one" (lines 1884). O'Hanlon accommodates both of them by suggesting:

```
1990    =Yeah Ok so the best of the old one ((hus-
1991    band nods yes)) (.hh) BUT (.2) see I don't
```

1992   want the old one back exactly (.2) cause I
1993   want the ol::d one (.1) with: a clear::
1994   commitment that he is here ((wife nods
1995   yes)) (1.0) So we'll take the old one (.2)
1996   new and r:r:rere:revise::ed or whatever the
1997   >revised edition< ((husband and wife both
1998   nod yes)) I want the second edition.

This presents the husband as having a clear commitment to the marriage. O'Hanlon ends the consultation by inviting the couple to answer questions from the audience who had been observing the session. The wife agrees and the husband follows suit.

THE AGENDAS OF THE WIFE AND HUSBAND

In the preceding section the agenda of the therapist was articulated. The therapist was maneuvering his talk and the couple's talk towards discussing solution-oriented behavior. What has not been discussed, however, are the agendas of the wife and husband. It is relevant to understand the agendas of the clients as well as the therapist. Without an understanding of how the couple's words and actions are being used to construct the conversation, the therapist would be unable to accomplish his/her goals. To simply assume that clients will comply with all interventions and suggestions would be an unsuccessful strategy to follow. Likewise, if the therapist could only randomly offer suggestions and randomly employ interventions, his/her strategies would likely fail miserably.

The relevance of knowing this information can be seen in Lewis Carroll's story of Alice playing croquet using flamingos as mallets. In the story, Alice is unable to hit the ball (a hedgehog) as each time she would swing the mallet, the flamingo would move its head. As Bateson (1972) points ˋut, "Alice's difficulty arises from the fact that she does not 'understand' the flamingo, i.e., she does not have systemic information about the 'system' which confronts her" (p. 449).

In this same manner, it is relevant for the therapist to understand the couple system with which he is interacting. What actions are the clients achieving in their talk and what meanings are they conveying? The previous analysis reveals many of the therapeutic moves of the therapist as he swings his mallet in this session. But, are there other interventions, or other ways to describe the process occuring in the session? Through understanding the couple's agendas, it will be possible to better describe the intricate processes of the session.

In this section, both the wife's and the husband's talk will be analyzed to determine the agendas that they are following. This analysis will answer the question of how the husband's and wife's actions are eliciting particular conversational patterns. After the agendas of all three participants have been described, these three threads will be woven together to reflect the contextually sensitive procedures that the therapeutic process follows. Following this, these procedures will be clearly articulated and demonstrated through the use of exemplars.

The Wife's Agenda

```
91 W:        . . . . ((swallows and turns towards hus-
92      band)) and I'm not saying this to hurt you
93      just to help us (.hhh) . . . .
```

The above statement by the wife, expressed early in the session, initially reflects her stated agenda for the session. This agenda has the wife presenting herself as motivated to make changes that will help both her husband and herself in the marriage. However, throughout the session, her utterances and actions achieve very different results and imply a different agenda.

As Watzlawick, Bavelas, and Jackson (1967) have noted, problems discussed in therapy not only describe events, but also convey information on an interactional level. Following her statement above (lines 92–93), the wife goes on to not only describe the events that have led up to seeing the therapist, but she is also making an interactional point. She is blaming the husband for what has happened. From an examination of the meaning of the wife's interactional moves, the agenda of the wife can also be described

```
112  this mean (.hh) meanwhile was eating away
113      at me inside ((therapist nods yes)) and my
114      heart was was breaking (.hhh) well it
115      reached to the point where we couldn't
116      live together and I I just wanted to stay
117      there cause I was on a maid shift I didn't
118      have anyone to watch my son ((therapist
119      nods yes)) and so (.hhh) about a a month
120      and half later after this had all (hhh)
121      been established and I knew there was a
122      relationship with my husband (.hhh) with
123      another girl then I moved into my mother's
124      house ((therapist nods yes)) and which
125      was extremely stressful (.hhh) ahm::
126  (1.0 pause)
```

In this segment, despite her statement that she is there to help the relationship, and not hurt the husband, the wife repeatedly highlights how much pain and hurt she feels. Additionally, the wife is also stressing how this hurt can be directly linked to the husband's actions and how she is not responsible for this problem. Following her comment that her heart was breaking (line 114), the wife states that the only reason she stayed living with him was because of her son (lines 115–118). Both of these statements are indirect methods that blame the husband for the problem (and her pain) and imply that she was unable to change the situation.

The wife (lines 121–123) reiterates that she knew of the relationship between the husband and another girl. She goes into this commentary with an audible exhale (line 120). Then, by using the relatively neutral word "relationship" instead of a stronger word like "affair," emphasizing the word "with," and inhaling after this comment, the wife is demonstrating her difficulty in describing the affair. This response indicates that the wife is having difficulty talking about this problem. This means that the topic being discussed is likely painful for the wife to talk about.

She follows up her comment by noting how <u>extremely</u> stressful (line 125) it was moving in with her mother. Juxtaposed with the prior comment about the husband's relationship, the wife is again stressing how injured and helpless she is from the husband's actions. Pointing out that she had to move into an extremely stressful situation emphasizes how bad the situation with her husband must be. The audible exhalation, the use of the extended particle "ahm::" and the long pause afterwards (lines 125–126) are devices that serve to emphasize the wife's discomfort in discussing her husband's behaviors.

In the 45-minute session, the wife repeatedly returns to describing her pain, noting the husband's behaviors, and thereby attributing blame to him. In the following segment, the wife presents a clear model of her view of her husband.

```
197  W:   = I think um (.5) there was a lot of lies a
198         lot of lot of just hateful things that
199         were done (.hhh) ((therapist nods yes))
200         and (.) he kinda pleads temporary insanity
201         which I think is a very poor excuse
202         ((therapist nods yes and no)) and I find
203         that hard to forgive him for that and =
204                                           [
205  T:                                       [*right*
206  W:   = (.hhh) it's I don't think it's fair that I
207         should be asked to just forgive him and
208         pretend like that's temporary insanity
209         ((therapist nods yes)) I don't you know
```

210   think that's asking a lot from me (.hhh)=
211   (hhhhhhhh)

In this segment the wife is clearly stating that she blames her husband for the "hateful things that were done." She will not forgive him for his excuse of temporary insanity. The pauses on line 197 and 200 are delay components that serve to emphasize the wife's discomfort in stating this view. Her audible inhalation (line 210) and extended audible exhalation (line 211) are responses that demonstrate the wife's difficulty in expressing these ideas, and draws attention to the discomfort she is experiencing relating these accounts.

The interactional agenda that the wife is actively pursuing is first developed in this segment. This agenda includes: (a) the husband has done terrible things, (b) the husband is responsible for all the problems that the family is experiencing, (c) the wife is suffering from the husband's actions, (d) the wife is not responsible for the problems. A fifth part of her agenda, that will be demonstrated in another segment, is that the wife is also trying to hurt or punish the husband for these problems.

That the husband has done terrible things is reflected by the wife's comments that "a lot of lot of just hateful things . . . were done" (lines 197–199) by him. That she perceives the husband as responsible for these actions is seen by the fact that he is trying to find excuses for the behaviors (lines 200–201). The wife's suffering is exemplified by her comment that to forgive him would be asking a lot from her (lines 209–211) and highlighted by the long, audible exhale. The wife's position, that she is not responsible for the problems, is illustrated by her statements that she is the one who has the perogative of granting forgiveness (lines 202–203 and 206–207). These four points and that the wife is actively pursuing this agenda can be demonstrated through her actions throughout the session.

The fifth part of the wife's agenda, that she is actively trying to hurt her husband, can be seen in the following segment.

730   . . . he's, I've said some
731   hurtful things, and I've I've I don't mean
732   not to hurt him but just to let him know:
733 *T:*   right ((nods yes))
734   and I know that it's gotta hurt him (.hh)

In this segment it appears at first that the wife may be mis-speaking when she states, "I don't mean not to hurt him" as the typical cliché is "I am not saying this to hurt him." The use of the double negatives gives a meaning that she does want to hurt him. Indeed, when compared to her earlier comments (lines 92–93) that "I'm not saying this to hurt you just to help us," it can be seen that she is aware of that cliché. That "she wants to hurt her husband" is the correct meaning for that statement (lines 731–732) can be demonstrated by two features. First, she does not attempt to repair or correct her statement to give it a more correct meaning. Secondly, she follows up her statement by emphasizing the point that she knows that "it's gotta hurt him (.hh)." The emphasis on the word "know" elaborates the wife's agenda as not only to blame her husband, but to also find ways to hurt him.

This understanding also allows for a new gloss on understanding her earlier comments on lines 91–93.

```
91  W:        . . . . ((swallows and turns towards hus-
92       band)) and I'm not saying this to hurt you
93       just to help us (.hhh) . . .
```

From a new reading of this statement it can be seen that the wife is having a difficult time expressing herself. She swallows before stating this, and then she inhales audibly upon completion. These two devices serve to show how painful it is for her to make this statement. From an understanding of her agenda, her comments (lines 91–93) can now be seen as ironic. As she tells her husband she is not saying this to hurt him, she is actually expressing how hurt she is. This is another example in which she blames the husband and leaves herself blameless.

That the wife does not hold herself accountable for any wrongdoing can be demonstrated in several segments from the session. The wife describes how a counselor she saw through work told her that she was emotionally stressed and depressed (lines 158–162). The wife then saw a psychiatrist for four or five sessions (lines 173–175) and she was not satisfied with either therapist.

```
175                          . . . . I
176   didn't get anything from her I needed
177   someone to wake me up to life and just say
178   you know >this is where you are at this is
179   what you have to do these are your goals<
180   ((therapist nods yes)) and and she just
181   kinda said "how do you feel about that?"
182   and "what are you doing?" ((therapist nods
183   yes)) and and you know an an it just it
184   didn't get me to where I wanted to go, I
185   needed someone to shake me and be alive
186   again=
```

In this segment the wife is normalizing her situation. She states that she just needed to be woken up and told what goals to strive for (lines 177–

179). She presents her problem as simply being not alive and active. It is a problem of omission or passivity, rather than anything wrong she actually committed. The implication of this position, tied in with the earlier statements, demonstrates how she is not responsible for their current problems. Indeed, her emphasis on her passivity (needing to be woken up) serves to further highlight the distinction of her husband's active responsibility for the problems.

Further demonstration of the wife's agenda of not being responsible for the problem can be seen in the deviant example when she does question her part in the problem.

```
1344   like we've talked about what drove him to
1345   her, and everything and (.hhh) and like
1346   she lived ((therapist nods yes)) on wel-
1347   fare she's a unwed mother she has a child
1348   of her of her own and everything (.hhh)
1349   but it was just it (.hh) she didn't
1350   require anything of him.
```

In this segment the wife is wondering perhaps what she may have done to "drive him to her" (lines 1344–1345). She points out that the girlfriend did not require anything of him. The implication of this position is that perhaps the wife did require too much of the husband. The segment would indicate that the wife might bear some responsibility for their problems. However, as the wife continues to expand on this topic she adds:

```
1370              and in my in my relationship (.hh) I
1371         mean I required him I said no dammit
1372         ((therapist nods yes)) you're not going
1373         out golfing tonight cause you have to =
1374              [
1375   T:            [right
1376   W:   = baby-sit cause I have to work or whatever. =
1377   T:   = You know tal::k with me: or whatever yeah,
1378         there was more pressure
1379                      [
1380   W:                   [So:: it was like it was
1381         you know I can I can see his point with
1382         that but I just still I get angry because
1383         he pleads temporary insanity with the the
1384         hurt that he had done me.
```

In this segment the wife states some of the actual demands that she places on her husband. Her example is that when she has to work, he has to babysit rather than play golf (lines 1372–1376). In the context of the session, this is an ironic example that serves more to place blame on the husband rather than involve the wife in irresponsible behavior. When the therapist formulates her position as the wife putting pressure on the husband, the wife interrupts the therapist (line 1380). She repeats herself several times (lines 1380–1382) as she searches for what she wants to say. Finally, she does state that she can see her husband's point, but she adds that she still gets angry over his excuse of temporary insanity.

What the wife has done is made the appearance that she does bear some responsibility for the problem, but she has presented it in such a manner that she can still maintain her innocence. In this segment, the wife has actually accomplished accepting responsibility in such a manner that it makes the husband look even more responsible (choosing golf over babysitting) for the problems, while she becomes less responsible (making reasonable requests that the husband does not comply with).

Another deviant example that demonstrates the wife's agenda can be seen in the following segments (lines 447–523). During the session when the therapist is trying to understand why she moved back with her husband, the wife first states that she moved back because the girlfriend called her up.

```
447  W:              [Well: the thing that did] it
448       to me is his girlfriend called me up and
449       she said "(Carrie) is it true that you're
450       going back with him" and and at this point
451       I I had not made the decision . . .
                  . . .
468  W:                             [yeah,
469       yeah ((unfolds arms)) and so so ah she
470       said "he called me and said he wouldn't
471       have anything to do with me and that it
472       was over with between us." And so I knew
473       this and obviously he had proven to me
474       (.hhh) that finally he was possibly gonna
475       drop her. =
476  T:   = So you saw some action from him and that's
477       what you needed to see? ((wife nods yes))
478                     [
479  W:                 [ye:ah:?
480  T:   some commitment (.hh) some action from him,
481       saying OK (.hh) at least he's moving in
482       this direction saying he wants (.hh) you
483       know he doesn't want that and he's ((wife
484       nods yes)) ge getting that (1.3) tossing
485       that away ehh you know avoiding that (.hh)
486       and saying *OK* I Would like this and then
```

487   you had to really say "(.hhh) alright I
488   seen some action now:: can:: (.) I: (.)
489   possibly:: (.2) (.hh) think about: getting
490   back together" And you and at that point
491   you said "OK (.1) I'm willing to try"
492   ((wife nods yes)) (1.0) OK, so you two
493   moved back together and you now you just had
494   this trip to New York, yes = "
495 W: = We ((shaking head no)) didn't want to move
496   back together. I don't think I really
497   ((therapist nods yes)) wanted to move back
498   together this was kinda pressured (.hhh)
499   my family has totally disowned me, my sis-
500   ter called me up ((therapist nods yes)) >I
501   have five brothers and sisters< and (.hh)
502   my parents are divorced I've been living
503   with my mother which was a high stress =

       . . .

507 W: = situation she's (.hh) like to discipline my
508   my son (therapist nods yes)) and he I
509   mean we were always beaten as kids we
510   always we never (.hhh) I mean if we did
511   anything wrong my mom beat the hell out of
512   us . . .

       . . .

519 W: [(It was and my) I
520   could see my son dealing with ((therapist
521   nods yes)) with what I dealt with as a kid
522   and I was like I can't do this to this
523   kid. =

In the first two segments above the wife begins by explaining that she moved back because the girlfriend calling her was evidence that the husband might possibly drop the girlfriend. This portrays the wife as possibly forgiving the husband. If this is indeed accurate, it would challenge the model that the wife's agenda is to blame the husband and not forgive him. However, as the therapist begins to clarify the wife's statements the wife begins to change this position. Her first response to the therapist (line 479) is a very weak agreement. As the therapist continues in his summary of what is happening for the couple, the wife gives agreement via head nods. However, on line 495, she finally jumps into the therapist's turn (as seen by the = sign) and corrects the therapist on why she moved back with her husband.

Her repairs (lines 495–503, 507–512 and 519–523) of her previous statement (lines 469–475) focus on the difficulties she was having living with her mother. The stress in living with her family was even worse than the stress she had had with her husband. She also expresses strong concerns for her son's well-being. The wife's added comments that she has five brothers and a sister and that her parents are divorced (lines 500–502) serve to further emphasize the severity of her family disowning her, that is, the larger the family, the greater the pain.

These three themes, being disowned by her family, her mother's beatings, and the concern for her son in that environment serve to offer a different explanation on why she returned to her husband. It can be seen that the situation with her mother was so terrible, moving back with her husband was "the lesser of two evils." The wife, in these segments, is again making a point that: (a) the pain and hurt she feels from her husband's actions are very strong, (b) he is responsible for her son being exposed to that abusive situation, and (c) she is not responsible for the problems.

Finally, that the wife is actively pursuing this agenda can be demonstrated in two ways. First, the multiple exemplars provided above indicate that the wife continuously seeks to push her point across. Secondly, near the end of the session, when the therapist asks if there is anything more either the wife or husband needs to add before they finish (lines 1766–1769), the wife's response demonstrates her tenacity. First, the wife responds:

```
1771  W:   ((Husband looks towards wife as if for her
1772         to answer)) *I I don't know* (2.1) *I
1773         think I gotten pretty much what I want out
1774         ((therapist nods yes and husband nods
1775         yes)) and I don't know*
1776  T:    *OK* (.hhh) =
1777  W:    = Then I asked him and that's what bothers me
1778         most ((folds arms over chest)) is just the
1779         trust in him (.hhh) =
1780  T:    = yeah right ((nodding yes, coughs)) =
1781  W:    = how to build that back that's what I have
1782         to do before I can do anything I I feel
1783         that's important like before I can go any-
1784         where ((unfolds arms from chest))
1785         (.hhh) is to get that trust back
```

When provided with the opportunity to finish the session, the wife first responds, albeit softly and tentatively, that she is satisfied with the session. The therapist accepts that (line 1776). However, the wife immediately (as seen by the = sign) launches back into not forgiving the husband. She states that until she can get trust for him she cannot go anywhere (lines 1781–1785). This return to her agenda, following a possible closing moment in the session, demonstrates the importance for the wife to express and pursue her agenda.

The Husband's Agenda

In constructing a model of the husband's agenda, some difficulties immediately arise. For the duration of the 45-minute session, the husband speaks remarkably less than either his wife or the therapist. He speaks on only 36 occasions, while the wife has 93 turns and the therapist 113 turns at speaking (excluding his acknowledgement replies of "yeah," "uh huh," "right," etc.). Many of the therapist's turns at speaking cover an expanse of over 100 lines and four-minutes stretches. Many of the wife's turns cover over 60 lines and three-minute stretches. The longest turns that the husband holds are no more than four lines and last less than 25 seconds. Many of his comments are even shorter than that time span.

In order to build a model of his agenda, it is useful to consider what the husband does not say in addition to what he does express. As will be illustrated, there are moments in the session when it is appropriate for the husband to speak, that he does not speak. These instances become useful in developing an understanding of his actions. In addition, the timing of his nonverbal communication, such as laughing and smiling, become relevant in understanding his agenda.

At first, the interactional agenda that the husband is pursuing appears to be almost a nonagenda agenda. It is almost as if he has no goals that he is pursuing in the session. However, on closer examination of his actions, it can be seen that the husband is attempting to stand on firm ground and maintain a low profile. His agenda appears to consist of: (a) avoid mistakes, (b) agree rather than disagree with either the therapist or his wife, (c) when unsure of what to say, say nothing. Simply put, the husband is trying to play it as safe as possible.

For example, the husband's first words in the session are in response to the therapist's request of "from either of you, whoever wants to start" (lines 31–32).

```
34  H:   ((looks towards wife)) You made the call you
35        could (.8) you want to talk first?
36        [
37  W:   [((laughter))
```

In examining the husband's answer, it can be seen that he changed how he wanted to express himself. He begins by taking the initiative and answering first. However, after his wife starts to laugh during his utterance of "could," he pauses .8 of a second in order to change his response. He then repairs his first few words by now asking her, "you want to talk first?" This appears to be a shift from the stronger statement of "you made the call you could talk first," to the more neutral request of, "do you want to talk first?"

If he had gone with the first choice, he would have expressed more of an assertive statement rather than a question. If pursued, the husband's comment would likely have followed a format of "since you (the wife) made the call, you brought us here, you should talk first," However, after the wife laughs, he changes his direction. It is possible that he perceived her laughter as a possible rejection or criticism of his beginning statement. Instead, he chooses to go with the more open, and safer request of, "you want to talk first?" This is expressed clearly as a question rather than a statement.

Many of the husband's responses in the session are safe or neutral acknowledgments that agree with either his wife or the therapist. On line 95, he says "I know, *I know*" to his wife's statement. On line 971, he agrees with the therapist's assessment of him as he says "I feel like that sometimes." Other examples (lines 714, 934, 1045, 1204, 1520, and 1899) can be found in the transcript where the husband provides short statements of agreement to either his wife or the therapist. Throughout the session, the husband also nods his head as a way of acknowledging agreement with his wife or the therapist.

Many times in the session, too, the husband waits to respond until he is sure of the appropriate response. For example, after the wife jokes about losing 56 pounds, the husband waits for the therapist to smile before he smiles.

```
139 W:   So, um, but I have lost 56 pounds? ((laugh-
140      ter)) since March ((laughter))
141  T:  That's good? that isn't ba:d? ((gestures to
142      the left and right, smiles, husband looks
143      at therapist and then husband smiles))
```

Another example occurs after the therapist uses humor to exaggerate the wife's decision to move back home.

```
425  T:  = what got you to make that decision >I
426      mean< >I just want to ask> ((wife puts her
427      hands to her hair and shakes her head no))
428      (you may be thinking)
429 W:   = ((laughter)) ( )
430  T:  ((Therapist puts his hands to his head))
432      (husband looks at wife and then husband
433      laughs)) . . . .
```

This lag response by the husband occurs at least six other times in the session (lines 391–392, 965, 1481–1485, 1636–1637, 1771–1775, and 1945–1947) where he laughs or smiles after either the therapist or his wife first signal that it is appropriate to laugh. These examples demonstrate that the husband is monitoring his actions as he is very careful not to respond inappropriately by laughing at something at which he should not be laughing.

The husband will take the initiative in answering questions when he thinks he knows the appropriate and correct response. Several times when the therapist poses questions looking for solution-oriented behaviors, the husband is the first to respond. For example, after the therapist has requested a situation from the couple of a time that the two of them had fun during this period of difficulty, the husband responds first.

```
322   Like we went to ah (name) Park (.4) ((wife
323   nods yes)) with our son during the middle
324   of that (.9) and I thought it was a won-
325   derful day.
```

This answer fits the therapist's criteria of a good time. However, as the husband expresses his thoughts, he leaves long pauses in his turn. These pauses allow him to monitor the reaction of the other two people, and thereby allow himself time to change his answer. In this segment, the wife nods agreement after his first pause (lines 322–323). The second pause (line 324) elicits no negative response, so the husband completes his thought. However, when the therapist then asks the wife if she would agree with the husband (lines 326–327), she says no. At this point, the husband does not pursue his answer, but rather, lets the therapist carry on the discussion with the wife. This demonstrates that while the husband is willing to offer answers that are helpful, if a problem arises over his response, he does not strive to push his point across.

Another segment that demonstrates this point occurs when the therapist is finding out from the wife if the husband's assurances to have her check up on him are to help her, or because he does not trust himself.

```
1633  W:   =(.hh) I'm like does he want me to check up
1634       on him because he (.) doesn't (.) trust
1635       himself or does he want me to check up on
1636       him to make me feel better? ((therapist
1637       nods yes)) (.hhh) you know =
1638  T:   = Let's ask him. ((gestures to the husband))
1639  W:   (hhh) I know my answer already.
1640  T:   Yeah:: what's the answer?
1641                      [
```

1642 *H:*   [I want I want you to
1643   check up on me so you'll feel better? =

In this segment, the obvious answer for the husband is to choose, "I want you to check up on me to help you feel better." The husband does select this as his answer. However, he hesitates in his response as he repeats "I want I want." This serves to allow him time to monitor the others for a reaction to see if he should change his answer. He then ends his statement with a rising inflection on "better." This makes his comment appear more as a question than a statement, as if he is not quite sure of his answer. This serves to demonstrate again that while the husband will answer questions when he thinks he knows the appropriate answer, he nonetheless tries to protect himself should he answer incorrectly. He is striving to maintain a safe position.

Further confirmation of the husband's agenda can be observed in instances when he does utter an inappropriate comment but he finds a method to repair his response. When asked by the therapist, "Is it done?" (line 215) in regard to the affair being over, the husband responds, "I want it to be done, yes" (line 220). This answer conveys two messages. One message is that ending the affair is out of his hands. He is not the one responsible for ending it, that is, "I would end it if I could, but I cannot." The other message in his statement of "I want it to be done, yes," is that the affair has not been terminated. His answer is not a safe response.

After the therapist rephrases his question, the husband responds:

226 (.hhh) (1.0) I would say it's ah 95 per-
227 cent over (.) ((therapist nods yes)) she
228 tries to contact me at work =

After an audible breath intake and a long pause, the husband clarifies that it is the girlfriend who has the responsibility to end the affair. The husband uses this long pause to consider how he will now answer the therapist's question. After a short pause (line 227), and a head nod by the therapist that he is on the right track of an appropriate answer, he adds that "she tries to contact me at work." This explanation helps to repair his earlier statement of "I want it to be done, yes" (line 220). His added explanation implies that the ex-girlfriend (and not he) is responsible for pursuing any contact, and the only contact with the ex-girlfriend is over the phone. When given the chance by the therapist to repair his earlier answer, the husband does elaborate on his first, inappropriate answer.

Another example of an inappropriate response and the repair by the husband, occurs on line 1135. The therapist has been talking about shared marital activities that the couple had been doing since coming back together.

```
1127  T:  Yeah:: do you have any shared activities =
1128          [                              ]
1129  W:           [It's only been a week so,
1130  T:   = anymore? I mean, no but I mean, as you've
1131       been sorta (.) coming back together or
1132       before what did you do either one?
1133  W:  We haven't really done anything he goes
1134       golfing and (.hhh)
1135  H:  And I enjoys basketballing again =
1136  W:  = yeah =
1137  H:  = and those are the things that keep person-
1138       ally that keep me going. ((therapist nods
1139       yes))
1140  T:  And you that's sorta the thing that's fun =
1141                       [
1142  H:               [But we
1143  T:   = for you?
1144  H:  Oh, yeah, but we use to enjoy, you know
1145       going to the show.
1146  T:  Oh movies, yeah you said movies was one of
1147       the things =
1148  H:   = We've rented movies ah and sat =
1149  W:                   (hhhhhhhh) ((wife shrugs))
1150                       [
1151  T:                   [Yeah
1152  H:   = and watched the movies but that's not the
1153       same thing as going =
1154  T:   = No, because the kid's ther::e and it's you
1155       know it's it's it's difficult
```

In this segment the focus of the therapist's question is on shared activities. The wife responds that they do not really have any shared activities as the husband goes golfing (lines 1133–1134). The husband then responds that he enjoys playing basketball too (line 1135). This answer is inappropriate to the context. As the husband adds that playing basketball is what "personally . . . keeps me going" (lines 1137–1138) he is again focusing on personal satisfaction rather than marital satisfaction, which is what the therapist's question was initially seeking. Indeed, it was personal satisfaction that led to some of the problems in the marriage in the first place.

When the therapist (line 1140) begins to question his answer, the husband quickly adds that they enjoy going to the movies too (lines 1144–1145). In fact, he interrupts the therapist (line 1141), in order to begin the repair of his earlier comments. As the husband continues to talk about renting movies (line 1148) the wife exhales audibly and shrugs her shoulders (line 1149). This becomes a signal to the husband that again his answer is not quite right. As the wife does this, the husband once again repairs his response. He adds that watching videos is not the same as going to the movies (lines 1152–1153). That this is the right answer is seen by the therapist's response on lines 1154–1155.

Another example of the husband responding inappropriately occurs when the wife is expressing her anger at him for his excuse of temporary insanity.

```
1380  W:              [So:: it was like it was
1381       you know I can I can see his point with
1382       that but I still I get angry because
1383       he pleads temporary insanity with the the
1384       hurt that he had done to me.
1385  T:   Sure right.
1386  W:   So=
1387  H:   =But I feel it all now too: you know, I
1388       didn't feel anything when I was doin that
1389       (.hhh) but now I every day I still=
1390                   [
1391  T:                [Yeah
1392  H:   =feel that.
1393  T:   Yeah, so you say I'm goin through some pain
1394       too OK so:: (.hh) alright (1.0) so (.4)
1395       the question is (.) what would it take to
1396       be ready to (.2) *put that ring on again*
```

In this segment the husband is wanting to demonstrate to the wife that he feels pain too. His statement, "But I feel it all now too: you know" (line 1387) is a way to tell the wife that he too shares her hurt. However, as he continues, he states that he did not feel anything at the time he was having the affair. This is not a safe answer. After an audible inhale, which provides him with time to reconsider his response, he adds that "now I every day I still feel that" (lines 1389 and 1392). While "anything" in line 1389 and "that" in line 1392 are ambiguous as to what they refer to, it is likely the husband is referring to the pain of being unfaithful and hurting his family. However, he is still hard pressed to repair his comment that he "didn't feel anything when I was doing that" (lines 1387–1388).

The therapist then speaks (line 1393) and supplies a meaning and a repair of the husband's use of "that" and "anything." The therapist sees it as representing pain that the husband is experiencing. The therapist then has several long pauses as he talks (line 1394). This would be a good opportunity for the husband to enter the conversation and further repair his previous statement. The husband, however, does not say anything. This is likely his way of playing it safe. Following the pauses (line 1394) the therapist changes the topic (lines 1394–1396), which is another indication that the husband's previous response was not on safe ground. This fits with the husband's agenda of better to be silent than wrong.

Another way to demonstrate the husband's agenda of better to be silent than wrong can be observed in those instances where he does not answer when it does seem appropriate for him to answer.

```
360  W:   . . . and I would call his work and he was
361        gone and I drove to her house and his car
362        was parked right there< (.hh) so
363                                     [
364  T:                                [right, ok] ((husband
365        shrugs shoulders)) So::, so but (.) . . .
```

In this segment the wife has just accused the husband of spending the night with the girlfriend. A likely response at this time by the husband could be an explanation. A response such as "we were just talking" or "that was a while ago and I'm not seeing her anymore" could help alleviate the wife's concerns. However, it is the therapist who responds to the wife. The husband shrugs his shoulders, which is almost an act of admission. As the therapist continues his response (line 365), there is an extended word, "so::" and a pause. Both of these markers are places that the husband could interject his explanation. The husband remains silent, however.

Another example occurs when the wife is talking about the husband's job as a orderly, and he is often interacting with girls.

```
1407  W:   =his his job is on (.hhh) his job is on call
1408        and he he gets phone calls and it's it's
1409        girls ((therapist nods half yes and no))
1410        that call because they he works he's a
1411        orderly and he works you know (.hhh) and=
1412                                         [
1413  T:                                     [right
1414  W:   =the girls call and say we need you=
1415                         [
1416  T:                     [so:
1417  W:   =someone's gotta go to the hospital and he
1418        has to go there.
1419  T:   So eventually if he if he really: you know
1420        if he's really fool:ing you *you'll find
1421        out.*
```

In this segment, the easy response, and perhaps expected response by the husband, is to explain that because he works with women, it does not mean he is having an affair with anyone. However, the husband instead chooses to play it even safer by saying nothing, rather than risking an incorrect response.

Another example of his selection of silence over risking an inappropriate response occurs when the therapist is challenging the wife about what would happen if the husband were to have another affair again.

```
1472  W:                          . . . . Right now I
1473       trust it a liddle (.3) b:::ut? (.3) maybe
1474       what would happen if he has another tempo-
1475       rary bout of insanity ((wife nods yes)) he
1476       no he would just go "OH >I'm insane
1477       again<" ( )
1478  W:   ((laughs)) see you later (I know)
```

In this segment it would be very appropriate for the husband to insist that he would not have another affair. This is an opportunity for him to present himself in a strong manner that he is now committed to his wife and family. However, his silence and lack of response further highlight his agenda of avoiding mistakes by being neutral and playing it safe.

THE THERAPIST AND COUPLE SYSTEM

At this juncture of the analysis, and understanding of the systemic pattern of the participants in the session can be seen. Through examining the agendas of the therapist, wife and husband, and observing how they interact and modify each other, a model of the triadic system has been developed. The therapist has become part of the system as he pursues his agenda to change the couple system. As has been demonstrated though, the wife also persistently pursues her agenda. Together, the wife, husband, and therapist are attempting to move the system in different directions, striving to accomplish different agendas. The next section will examine the interactive weave of the three participants and examine how the therapist, as one member of the triadic system, attempts to impact the system by guiding the conversation in a particular direction.

THE DESCRIPTION OF A CLASS OF INTERVENTIONS

The Interactive Weave

In the preceding sections the agendas of the therapist, wife, and husband were examined. The therapist, per his writings (O'Hanlon, 1989; O'Hanlon

& Weiner-Davis, 1989; O'Hanlon & Wilk, 1987) and as seen in the transcript, is actively pursuing an agenda of changing the clients' perceptions from focusing on problem-oriented behaviors to focusing on solution-oriented behaviors. The wife's agenda includes demonstrating that the husband is responsible for her suffering and all the terrible things he has done, that she is not responsible for these problems, and that not only will she not forgive him, but she wants to hurt him too. The husband's agenda includes adopting a posture of playing it safe and minimizing his interactions in order not to do or say anything that may lead to a conflict.

In weaving these strands together and examining how these three agendas interact with each other, it can be seen that the therapist and wife are at cross-purposes in their pursuits of different agendas. They are both striving to control the conversation of the session in a specific direction and towards a particular outcome. The therapist is directing the talk towards solutions and resolution, while the wife's aim is for blame and continuation of getting the husband to take greater responsibility for the problem.

While the therapist and wife are clearly pursuing different agendas, the husband plays a more ambiguous role. The wife's and therapist's moves become strategies to define the husband's role. Has the husband made a mistake, and is he ready to pursue a positive and stable life with his wife and son, or is he a person that cannot be trusted, and may revert at any moment towards instability? The husband, for his part, is striving to be perceived as trusted and reliable, but he keeps saying things that make his role unclear.

Thus, each person in the session is following an agenda that interacts with the other participants in such a manner that their individual agendas are both created out of the interactions as well as help create the interaction. The first section of this chapter was an analysis of the therapist's major tactics in the therapy (his swinging of the flamingo mallet). There has been little discussion of the more contextually sensitive interactive moves that the therapist follows in adjusting and calibrating his talk to accommodate the agendas of the other participants in the conversation. This last section will examine those contextually sensitive moves that O'Hanlon uses in pursuing his therapeutic agenda.

Pursuing a Solution-oriented Response

In considering the contextually sensitive moves that O'Hanlon uses in the session, the image of a tapestry becomes a useful metaphor. What holds a tapestry together are the cross-threads, or cross weaves, that bind the major strands in a particular pattern. When the tapestry is finely constructed, these cross threads need to accommodate the various threads of the tapestry and conform to their different contours, while minimizing their own appearance. Depending on how well these cross-threads are stitched will also determine the tightness of the weave. Indeed, the integrity of the pattern of a tapestry depends on the effectiveness of these subtle cross-stitches.

Likewise, an effective therapy session will have effective cross-stitching in order to develop a tight pattern that will incorporate the various agendas of the different participants. These cross-stitch threads help prevent the session from unravelling. The major threads that compose this consultation session include O'Hanlon's strategies, that is, presupposing change, multiple-choice questions, normalizing the problem, and so on, combined with the agendas of the wife and husband.

The major cross-threads that O'Hanlon uses to maintain the integrity of his agenda are the procedures of pursuing specific responses from the clients. While a speaker pursuing a response from the listener is common to ordinary conversations, O'Hanlon is using this procedure in a highly sophisticated manner. As Pomerantz (1987) notes, in ordinary conversations, "If a speaker performs an action that solicits a response" (p. 152) and he/she does not receive the expected response, the speaker has two options. The speaker can abandon his/her attempt to elicit a particular response, or the speaker can pursue the desired response. O'Hanlon, in this session, diligently and consistently pursues specific responses from the couple in order to keep the essence of the conversation highly focused towards solutions.

If the speaker chooses to pursue a response to his/her assertion, Pomerantz (1987) notes three major procedures that the speaker can follow to elicit the desired response. If the listener is unclear of a reference, the speaker can review his/her assertion and clarify the reference. If the listener is unclear of the facts of a situation, or has different assumptions about the incident than those of the speaker, the speaker can go over the facts upon which the information is based. The third procedure occurs when the listener does not support or agree with the speaker. In this situation, the speaker can review and evaluate his/her assertions, and if they are wrong or overstated in some manner, modify what he/she had asserted (pp. 152–153).

Each of the above methods described by Pomerantz (1988) is designed to elicit a specific response. O'Hanlon doggedly pursues not simply specific responses, but a class of responses, in this session. He is pursuing those responses that follow a logical format which entail a solution-oriented reality. These responses are of a class of actions (verbal and nonverbal) that imply that the husband and wife are perceiving/acting in such a manner that supports a solution focus rather than a problem focus.

O'Hanlon's pursuit towards creating a specific solution-oriented conversation provides the major cross threads that bind the session into a particular pattern. O'Hanlon used the above pursuit procedures (as described by Pomerantz) as well as other procedures to modify the flow of the conversation until he received the type of response (typically a solution-oriented description) for which he was looking.

O'Hanlon's Pursuit Procedures

In an analysis of the session relative to how O'Hanlon would handle problematic occurrences and pursue the class of solution-oriented responses, nine procedures are described. These procedures include: (a) pursuing a response over many turns, (b) overlapping his talk with the husband or wife in order to get his turn, (c) clarifying unclear references, (d) (re)formulation, or going "over with the recipient the facts and information upon which he or she based the assertion" (Pomerantz, 1984, p. 153), plus, adding new facts from which to evaluate a shared understanding of the event, (e) offering a candidate answer (Pomerantz, 1988), (f) modifying his assertions until he received the response he was seeking, (g) ignoring the recipient's misunderstanding or rejection of his assertion, and continuing as if his assertion was accepted, (i) posing questions or possible problems and then answering these questions himself (instead of letting the couple speak for themselves), (j) using humor to change the topic from a problematic theme back to the topic that he is pursuing.

These nine procedures will first be explicated through the use of different exemplars from the session. Following this, an extended exemplar from the session will be analyzed to demonstrate how all nine procedures were used in the session.

(a) *Pursuing a response over many turns* is the procedure whereby O'Hanlon would persistently seek particular responses regardless of how long it would take until he elicited those responses. For example, on line 584 O'Hanlon first uses the strategy of utilizing and normalizing the wife's doubts. He tells the wife to keep and include her doubts and concerns rather than act as if she does not have any doubts. This is his strategy of striving to break the wife's pattern that for every time she feels any doubts about the husband, it must mean that there is a problem in their relationship.

He repeats this request many times throughout the session. He tells her to "include (.) . . . the doubts:" on lines 605–607 as well as on lines 696–697, and 704 (among other segments in the session). Towards the end of the session, O'Hanlon is still pursuing this agenda of reminding the wife to include her doubts (as seen on lines 1841–1842, 1844–1845, 1847–1848, and 1924–1928). He finally elicits a response from the wife which utilizes and normalizes her doubts as she says:

1939 *W:* ((laughing)) I go do you do you do I drive
1940   you crazy bringing her up everyday and he
1941   says (.hhh) he says well to tell you the
1942   truth I don't think about her until you
1943   <u>bring her up</u> ((laughing))

This segment has the wife laughing at herself in the way she constantly expresses her doubts by asking the husband about the girlfriend. O'Hanlon has finally elicited a response in which the wife does not view her doubts as necessarily being an obstacle to resolving her marriage. O'Hanlon has pursued this type of response over half the session and many turn takings until he finally elicited the targeted response.

(b) *Overlapping his talk with the husband or wife in order to get his turn* is the procedure by which O'Hanlon would interrupt the other speakers in order to disrupt their train of thought and express his own views. This procedure is similar to the "therapeutic interruption" strategy described by O'Hanlon and Wilk (1987). It is used to persistently pursue a particular class of topics as well as give the therapist a turn to express his views. In using this procedure, O'Hanlon would only continue an overlapped turn if the other speaker would stop talking. If the other speaker continued his/her turn, O'Hanlon would cease trying to overlap his/her talk (for the moment) and try again. In this manner, O'Hanlon is diminishing the obtrusive nature of the interruption.

For example, O'Hanlon states, "So eventually if he if he really: you know if he's really fool:ing you *you'll find out*" (lines 1419–1421). O'Hanlon, with this statement, is attempting to disrupt the wife's constant vigil of mistrusting her husband as he tries to convince her that she will find out if her husband should have an affair again.

He pursues this agenda with the wife through 14 turns (from lines 1422 to 1467). During this sequence, on six occasions the therapist either overlaps the talk of the other speaker (as seen by the [marker), or quickly attaches his words onto the other person's word before he/she can utter anything more (as seen by the = sign). He finally elicits a response of "uh umm" (line 1467) from the wife. While this is not a strong response by the wife, O'Hanlon has succeeded in developing his line of thinking. He then goes into an extended turn (lines 1468–1574) expanding his point. In this turn he continues to pursue the topic of developing trust as he offers the analogy of an elevator falling and learning to get back into it again.

(c) *Clarifying unclear references* is the procedure of clarifying a previous statement in order to achieve a common understanding of the assertion. An example of this procedure can be seen when the therapist asks, "what activities did you used to do or have you done recently since you've been sortof moving back together?" (lines 1123–1125). O'Hanlon, with this question, is eliciting examples from the wife of solution-oriented behaviors. The wife responds, "together?" (line 1126) as she is unclear about what O'Hanlon means by his question.

The therapist clarifies that he means "shared activities" (line 1127). The wife, overlapping O'Hanlon's answer, replies, that "it's only been a week" (line 1129) since they have been back together. This response indicates that the wife's understanding of his question focuses only on recently shared activities, rather than any activities they had done earlier. Her response is that because it has been less than a week, they have not had time to do things together.

The therapist then further clarifies his question as he asks, "I mean, no but I mean, as you've been sorta (.) coming back together or before what did you do either one?" (lines 1130–1132). While the wife replies "we haven't really done anything" (line 1133), and (at this juncture of the conversation) does not give the answer that O'Hanlon is pursuing, the therapist has clarified his question such that the wife now understands what type of information he is seeking.

(d) *(Re)formulation* (Davis, 1984) is the procedure whereby O'Hanlon would transform the facts of a previous assertion into something different. This is in contrast to merely clarifying previous information. This is done with the intent of achieving a shared understanding based on the transformed assertion. This procedure is analogous to the strategy of "summarizing with a twist." Through the process of (re)formulation O'Hanlon would change the meaning of an earlier event to provide it with a new meaning that would be more suitable to achieving his agenda. Several times in the session the therapist would (re)formulate the husband's statements in order to "repair" them from eliciting his wife's blame.

For example, the husband states about the affair, "I want it to be done, yes" (line 220) and "I would say it's ah 95 percent over (.) she tries to contact me at work=" (lines 226–228). O'Hanlon responds by saying:

```
229    =Ok, so from your side you said ok I want to
230    put this thing back together ((wife and
231    husband nod yes)) do what I can to put it
232    back together (.hh) ((husband nods yes))
233    she still sometimes tries to ahm get some
234    contact with ((husband nods yes)) you as
235    much as possible you (.8) (.hh) you've
236    been shoving it to the side ((gestures to
237    the right)) ((husband nods yes)).
```

O'Hanlon begins his response by quickly cutting into the husband's turn (as seen by the = sign) and saying "=Ok, so from you side you said . . ." (line 229). The words "ok" and "so" and the phrase "from your side" are

all markers that identify his forthcoming statements as a summary or formulation of the prior turn by the husband. O'Hanlon, however, then begins
his (re)formulation by crediting the husband as "wanting" to put the marriage back together. This is a shift from wanting the affair to be over to
wanting the marriage to be better. He repeats this idea twice for added
emphasis. The therapist then puts the onus of blame on the girlfriend ("she
tries to ahm get some contact with you," lines 233–234), which is a move
to shift the blame and responsibility from the husband, onto the girlfriend.
He then adds that the husband is "shoving it to the side" (line 236). As he
delivers this (re)formulation O'Hanlon is receiving head nods of agreement
from both the husband and the wife.

In this sequence the therapist has effectively repaired, or (re)formulated
the husband's comments (lines 220 and 222–224), which implied the affair
may be continuing. The new formulation implies that the affair is over. A
little later in the session, O'Hanlon further (re)formulates his formulation
(lines 229–237) of the husband's response as he paraphrases the husband
as having stated, "fo:r you know all: of the things that I *did* and I (.hh) I
admit: >I was wrong and it was crazy and all this stuff<" (lines 284–286).
In this second (re)formulation O'Hanlon further alters the husband's stated
position into an even stronger statement, admitting his part of the responsibility. Through adjusting the facts of the husband's previous assertions,
O'Hanlon is developing a new basis from which to pursue his agenda.

(e) *Offering a candidate answer* is a common method of eliciting information (Pomerantz, 1988). It is a procedure in which the person asking a question incorporates a likely answer in the question. Pomerantz (1988) notes
that when speakers use a candidate answer in "their inquiries, they give
the co-interactants models of the types of answers that would satisfy their
purposes" (p. 366) as they "shape the 'context' of the inquiry" (p. 370).
O'Hanlon would offer candidate answers in his questions in order to elicit
a particular response, and as a method to maintain the focus of his agenda.

This procedure is similar to "multiple choice questions," but it is slightly
different. Offering a candidate answer entails the therapist carefully choosing what candidate answers to include in the question. Offering choices that
are too different from the client's agenda will likely lead to a rejection.
Offering a candidate answer not only offers choices to the client, but it
reflects the therapist's understanding of the client's situation.

In the following segment, O'Hanlon is in the process of repairing the
husband's turn (lines 1387–1388). The husband's remarks could easily be
interpreted by the wife as meaning that he felt no remorse during the time
of his affair. By changing topics as he poses several questions, the therapist
can both pursue his agenda of eliciting solution-oriented behaviors from the
wife as well as interrupt her likely response of blaming the husband for his
response.

```
1387  H:    = But I feel it all now too: you know I
1388        didn't feel anything when I was doin that
1389        (.hhh) but now I every day I still =
1390                              [
1391  T:                          [Yeah
1392  H:    = Feel that.
1393  T:    Yeah, so you say I'm goin through some pain
1394        too OK so:: (.hh) alright (1.0) so (.4)
1395        the question is (.) what would it take to
1396        be ready to (.2) *put that ring on again*
1397        (2.0) Will it tak:e (1.2) more communica-
1398        tion? (.1) will it take more time? (.8)
1399        How:: can (.) he sho:w you (.2) tha:t
1400        he's really committed this >time? is<
1401        there a way that you can think of that he
1402        can show you or again will it be time?
1403        (.hhh)
1404  W:    (.hhh) I think it's gonna be time . . .
```

In this turn, O'Hanlon first acknowledges the husband's statement by noting that he is going through some pain too. Next, using pauses and several introduction markers (line 1394), O'Hanlon sets the tone for changing topics. On lines 1395–1396 he poses a question to the wife of "what would it take to be ready to (.2) *put that ring on again?*" After a two-second pause, O'Hanlon offers several candidate answers to the wife. Will it be "more communication" or "more time" (lines 1397–1398). Both of these answers are within the class of solution-oriented behaviors. He then poses still another question to the wife, and offers a possible answer of "will it be time?" (line 1402). The wife responds by going with the answer of "it's gonna be time" (line 1404).

In this sequence, O'Hanlon, in order to avert the wife's possible pursuit of her own agenda, pursues a change of topic instead. Following the husband's questionable response, O'Hanlon changes the topic by posing a question to the wife. He offers candidate answers to her and then poses another question. He again offers a candidate answer to the question. The wife responds to the therapist's series of questions and answers by accepting his choice of an answer and thereby allows a change of topic.

(f) *Modifying his assertion until receiving the desired response* is the procedure in which O'Hanlon would change or adjust what he was saying until he elicited the desired response from the other person. In the example below, O'Hanlon is seeking any objects that the husband might have from the girlfriend that can be used for a ritual.

The therapist began asking for something physical that can be used as a "concrete symbol" on line 1564. Through 11 turns he does not elicit an answer that will supply an object for the ritual. O'Hanlon then says, "so maybe there's nothing physical like that" (lines 1612–1613). The wife agrees, "I don't think so" (line 1616) and O'Hanlon then modifies his request.

```
1617   ahm (.4) I ah another thing that I've sug-
1618   gested with people maybe you'll come
1619   across something and then you'll have
1620   a letter or something and then you'll have
1621   one of those things ((wife nods yes)) so:
1622   sav:e it and burn it or bury it
```

Following this modification, (rather than pursuing do you have anything now, O'Hanlon is suggesting that she may find something later), the wife recalls having a $48.00 rose bill with the girlfriend's name on it. This response fits the therapist's original question, and allows him to pursue his agenda.

(g) *Ignoring the listener's misunderstanding or rejection of his assertion* is the procedure by which the therapist ignores rival agendas and follows his own line of pursuit. This is comparable to O'Hanlon and Wilk's (1987) strategy "to deliberately ignore certain communications" (p. 83) uttered by the client in order to introduce doubt into his/her way of thinking. In other words, if the wife makes an assertion that does not fit his solution focused agenda, O'Hanlon, at times, will act as if the comment was not uttered and continue on with his own line of thought.

In the following segment the wife is expressing her concern regarding the husband's urgency to put his wedding band back on (lines 1279–1282).

```
1279  W:      [But see that's what we were talking
1280          about, we don't wear our wedding bands
1281          (.8) (.hhh) an:d he's: in a hurry to put
1282          his wedding band on: and he says=
1283                  [
1284  T:                      [right
1285  W:     =you know I wanna I wanna be married now.
1286                  [
1287  T:                      [That may be part of
1288          the ceremony (.1) This is good. =
1289  W:     =Yea::h? But then it's like (.hhh) it's
1290          like that's fine but we put these on ONE
1291          other time:: you know, and it's
1292          like yeah, and it's        yeah=
1293          [                            ]
1294  T:    [And di:d they mea:::n anything did it mean
1295          any anything so]
```

```
1296  W:   = proven to me 8 years that nothing you know =
1297                            [
1298  T:                        [good
1299  W:   = and I find a real hard time dealing with
1300         tha:t. (.hhh) =
1301  T:   = good, so don't put em on before you're
1302         ready ((wife nods yes)) (1.0) Now: (1.0)
1303         HOW:: will you know you're ready?
```

On line 1285 the wife expresses her concern for her husband's impatience to be married now. She perceives his impatience as a problem. O'Hanlon, however, overlapping the wife's turn, treats the husband's urgency as a resource that can be incorporated into the ceremony (lines 1287–1288). Indeed, he emphasizes "This is good" (line 1288).

The wife (lines 1289–1292) quickly responds however (as seen by the = sign) to clarify the therapist's response. She begins with questioning his remark ("Yea::h?"), and then states "it's like (.hhh) it's like that's fine" (lines 1289–1290). This is likely a response to the therapist's remark that the husband's urgency can be used in the ceremony. Her repeating "it's like (.hhh) it's like" is a device to agree partially with the therapist's remark, while implying that there is more to the husband behavior than the therapist understands. She continues with more information to clarify why this is indeed a problem (lines 1290–1291). Her emphasis on "but we put these on ONE other time:: you know" stresses that putting the wedding rings on the first time was not meaningful and did not prevent the affair.

O'Hanlon, overlapping the wife's turn, responds with the ambiguous statement, "And di:d they mea:::n anything did it mean any anything so" (lines 1294–1295). This statement could either mean that the husband putting the ring on 8 years ago did not mean anything (agreeing with the wife's assertion), or the fact that it did not mean anything then is now useful information.

The wife accepts the first meaning of this statement as she says, it's "proven to me 8 years that nothing you know" (line 1296). O'Hanlon however, continues by saying, "good, so don't put em on before you're ready" (lines 1301–1302). He has continued with his meaning that the insincerity of 8 years ago can now be changed, rather than signifying that it would still be a mistake to exchange rings. O'Hanlon, then asks, "HOW:: will you know you're ready" (line 1303), confirming the meaning of his assertion, that the topic of the wedding band is useful gist for a solution. Through being deliberately dense rather than perceptive of the wife's statements, O'Hanlon has ignored the wife's interpretation of the meaning of the rings and continued as if his assertions were both accurate and accepted by the wife.

(h) *Posing questions or possible problems and then answering these questions himself* is the procedure whereby O'Hanlon would anticipate possible problematic interruptions and formulate possible answers for either the husband or wife. In this way he could both maintain his turn and pursue his agenda by attributing information to the wife or husband.

In the following segment, O'Hanlon is pursuing the issue of whether the wife still loves her husband or not, and whether they can find reasons to live together. O'Hanlon is attempting to challenge the wife to move past simply blaming her husband, and to consider her options. This, again, is a pursuit for solution-oriented behaviors rather than problematic behaviors. In this segment, O'Hanlon is in the middle of telling a story of other couples that he has seen.

644 T: . . . "Is there
645   any light down there now? cause I can't
646   really you know like I'm saying I'm not
647   sure I lov:e him anymore" (.hhh) But the
648   way you said it is really like "is:: there
649   anything underneath that, ((wife nods
650   yes)) that manure (.) or is there not. I
651   mean do I really still love him? ((wife
652   nods yes)) >There's a lot of water under
653   the bridge I don't know whether I do or
654   not< (.hhh) ahh it's: more convenient to
655   go back at this point and it's I feel bad:
656   saying that because it sounds so you know,
657   financial or heartless, ((wife nods yes))
658   but in one way (.hh) that is the truth I
659   mean it's easier to raise your kid
660   toge:ther, it's easier financially, ((wife
661   nods yes)) it's easier in terms of living
662   situations . . .

On line 644 O'Hanlon poses the question "Is there any light down there now?" This question is ambiguous as it is unclear if it refers to the story that he just told the couple or is he asking them if they still have love for each other. This ambiguity allows him to continue without either the husband or wife needing to respond. He then adds "you know like I'm saying I'm not sure I lov:e him anymore" (lines 646–647). This line appears to be directed to the wife, but there is still some ambiguity as O'Hanlon continues with "is:: there anything underneath that, that manure" (lines 648–649). This comment seems to be a continuation of the story.

As O'Hanlon continues his turn, he poses more questions that become clearly directed to the wife, "do I really still love him" and "I don't know whether I do or not" (lines 650–654). He phrases these questions as if the wife herself is asking them. He then continues by answering the questions for the wife himself (lines 654–666). In this segment, the therapist offers various rationales for the wife, which include going back to the husband because she loves him, going back because of their son or not going back to her husband.

All of these possible answers address the wife's doubts, but in a manner that directs her to make a choice rather than simply dwell in her doubts. Through posing questions and speaking for the wife, O'Hanlon is raising the possibility that regardless of the wife's feelings for the husband, she needs to make a choice regarding her plan of action. In this manner, O'Hanlon is getting the wife to focus on goals rather than problems.

(i) *Using humor to change the topic from a problematic theme back to a solution-oriented topic* is the procedure whereby O'Hanlon would disrupt problem talk (or possible problem talk) by the wife or husband and shift the focus of the conversation towards a new direction. This procedure is similar to O'Hanlon and Wilk's (1987) use of humor (pp. 174–177). O'Hanlon and Wilk, however, tend to describe this strategy more as a way to entertain the client and therapist. The use of humor as a procedure to change the topic of the conversation is a specific procedure used to disrupt talk and change the focus of the conversation.

In the following sequence the husband has just responded to the wife's anger at his inability to express his feelings. The husband responds, "(well) I'm I'm usually the last: to know how I feel" (lines 924–925). His response is problematic in that it could generate more anger from the wife for his lack of sensitivity to her feelings of the hurt and pain he has caused the family. O'Hanlon responds:

```
926  T:   ((laughter)) (yea:h right) ((slaps knee))
927        It's like, "huh:: I won::der ho:w ((wife
928        laughs)) I do: fee:l? ah::? goo::d ques-
929        tion::" an:d so:: ah so during those con-
930        versations though that you've had, those
931        you know sitting down every night (.hh)
932        have you been able to get a little more to
933        that?
934  H:   Sometimes.
```

In this segment O'Hanlon takes the husband's comment as a joke. He begins by laughing, saying "yea:h right" and slapping his knee (line 926). He then exaggerates the husband's comment through the use of the word "huh" and extending each word as he pronounces them (lines 927–928). The wife starts laughing as O'Hanlon pursues this humorous exaggeration of the husband's response.

O'Hanlon then shifts topics as he says, "an:d so:: ah so during those conversations though that you've had" (lines 929–930). These "conversations" are in reference to a remark that the wife had made on lines 720–721, over 16 turns earlier, when she mentioned times that she and her husband were able to communicate their feelings to each other. Following O'Hanlon's turn of humor and topic shifting, the husband agrees that "sometimes" (line 934), they have gotten closer in discussing feelings during these conversations. O'Hanlon effectively averted a possible problem and diverted the talk towards a solution focused conversation.

An Example that Incorporates all Nine Procedures

In the following segment, divided into three parts, the above nine procedures were used by the therapist to pursue a particular response.

```
304  T:   things: went ok like you either had
305        ((therapist counts on his fingers) a really
306        good discussion your communication was:
307        good* umm and or (.2) you know, th times
308        (1.0) when things were jus:t (1.1) better
309        for some inexplicable reason can you
310        remember a moment in there, an evening,
311        ah: day, (.hh) when actually (.2) the two
312        of you felt like (.1) *wow you know* > for
313        some reason we didn't have a conflict or
314        we had a conflict and we worked it out
315        very satisfactorily for both of us< (.hhh)
316        or we just had one of these pleasant
317        interactions that was really good, ca tell
318        me about one of those times cause I'm
319        going to try and ah (.hh) er find in there
320        some pieces that we can use to maybe (.1)
321        ah build something else for the future.
322  H:   Like we went to ah (name) park (.4) ((wife
323        nods yes)) with our son during the middle
324        of that (.9) and I thought it was a won-
325        derful day.
326  T:   Ok, would you agree that that was a pretty
327        good day?
328  W:   No, >because I knew she was still there.<=
329  T:   =Ok, so that
330              [
331  W:   [>we spent the entire day together
332        and he kept saying I want this back
333        ((therapist nods yes)) I want my family
334        back and I am so sorry for all the hurt
335        I've done< ((therapist nods yes)) (.hhh)
```

```
336        and on the way home I said does she know
337        that you're with me today that we went on
338        this family daytrip, and he goes are you
339        going to call her and tell her, he was
340        scared to death I was going to call her
341        and tell her (.hhh) He did this (.) quite
342        a few times during our relationship where
343        he would say, (.hhh) >" God I want all this
344        back and I am so sorry I dropped it"<
345        (.hhh) but then I would sa
346                           [
347  T:                        [But then other
348        things that he said made you sort ah think
349        is he rea:lly committed to
350                           [
351  W:                        [Well she lives on
352        the sam:e (.1) >street as I do< and I =
353                           [
354  T:                        [right
355  W:  = would like we would spend an evening
356        together at his parents' house and then I
357        would I would go home (.hh) and put my son
358        to sleep and he (.1) >I would call the
359        house and he was gone ((therapist nods
360        yes)) and I would call his work and he was
361        gone and I drove to her house and his car
362        was parked right there< (.hh) so
363                           [
364  T:                        [right, ok] ((husband
365        shrugs shoulders)) So::, so but (.) that's
366        the ki:nd of thing you w::ould like to do
367        in the future you know like sp sp spend
368        like you just went ah where did you go over
369        to, New York?
```

This long segment begins with O'Hanlon posing a question to the couple as he offers candidate answers (lines 304–321). In this segment, the therapist is suggesting possible answers to the couple in order to elicit a particular class of responses. He suggests such answers as "a good discussion," "communication was good," "things were just better for some inexplicable reason," "an evening," "a day," "no conflict," "a conflict was worked out," or "a pleasant interaction" (lines 304–317). Following the therapist's pursuit through offering a candidate answer, the husband does offer an appropriate answer, going to the park (lines 322–325), which fits in the class of solution-oriented behaviors.

However, the wife rejects (line 328) O'Hanlon's formulation (lines 326–

327) of the husband's description of a good day. O'Hanlon tries to insert a comment into the conversation as soon as the wife starts to explain her rejection of the husband's response. The wife makes a quick response (as seen by the > < marks) to start her explanation (line 328) and O'Hanlon attempts to join in before she can start up again (as seen by the = sign). The wife, however, overlaps the therapist's talk to continue her explanation (line 330).

As the wife continues her turn O'Hanlon would nod his head occasionally. The wife continues for 14 lines until the therapist overlaps her turn again (line 346). In this overlap, O'Hanlon is attempting to formulate the gist of what the wife is saying. He is going over the information of her assertion, as he then (re)formulates her assertion, adding, "But then other things that he said made you sort ah think is he rea::lly committed to . . ." (lines 347–349).

This (re)formulation is designed to sum up the wife's turn by first agreeing with her assessment of the husband's lack of commitment, but then, add an element of ambiguity or doubt through the emphasis on the word "really." If the wife accepts this (re)formulation, it changes the assumptions of her assertion and it will likely (a) allow the therapist to get his turn back, and (b) allow him to resume his earlier pursuit of solution-oriented behaviors. The wife, however, chooses to continue her turn (lines 351) as she overlaps O'Hanlon's turn (line 350) in order to further elaborate on the husband's immoral behavior.

In pursuit of his agenda, O'Hanlon overlaps the wife's turn (line 363) before she can clearly formulate and articulate her own position. As the wife is saying "so," which is typically a start of a formulation, the therapist begins with his own formulation (lines 364–369). O'Hanlon's formulation begins with "right, ok" which first acknowledges the wife's turn. He then continues with further markers of a formulation, "So::, so but (.)" which serve to emphasize a change in the topic. He then returns to the question he posed eight turns earlier (lines 326–327) ignoring the wife's rejection as if it had not been expressed.

His comment, "that's the ki:nd of thing you w::ould like to do in the future" (lines 365–367) bear no reference to the wife's previous four turns (from lines 328–362), which rejected his first try for the answer he wanted, and instead, is referenced to his earlier question (lines 326–327). He then asks a question of clarification, "ah where did you go over to, New York?" (lines 368–369). This question supplies a candidate answer as he also diverts the wife's attention towards clarifying the husband's earlier statement (nine turns earlier, on lines 322–325), rather than questioning O'Hanlon's shift in topic.

To recapitulate, thus far in this segment, O'Hanlon has pursued his agenda through offering candidate answers to his question, overlapping the wife's talk, going over the facts of his assertions by (re)formulating the wife's assertions, overlapping the wife's talk again, ignoring the wife's turns which reject his assertion and continuing as if his assertion (eight turns earlier) had been accepted, and shifting the wife's attention by offering a candidate answer to a statement presented nine turns earlier.

The following segment begins with the therapist getting an answer to his diverting question of "ah where did you go to, New York?" O'Hanlon then continues to pursue a more elaborate solution-oriented response from the wife.

```
370  W:   New York, *yeah*. ((husband and wife both nod
371        yes))
372  T:   ((looks at husband)) And so that that kind
373        of thing is something you'd like to do
374        more of ((husband nods yes)) (.hh) those
375        family things: that: would be nic:e ((hus-
376        band nods yes)) and that was nice for you:
377        (.hh) ((looks at wife)) and it sort of got
378        washed out for you by the knowledge ((wife
379        nods yes)) that she was there in the back-
380        ground and he still was (.hh) his energy
381        was still there in some ways (.hhh) how
382        about then, then I need to ask you if
383        ((looks at husband)) maybe ask you some
384        more but (.8) (.hh) ((looks at wife)) any-
385        times that it was:: good in terms of what
386        you perceived (1.0) Any moments that were
387        good, even though you knew that that was
388        happening any moments or any evenings or
389        any days that you thought were good?
390            (.9 pause)
391  W:   ((Husband looks at wife to let her reply))
392        Not really because we really didn't =
393            [
394  T:       [ok
395  W:   =communicate and like the only time we =
396            [
397  T:       [I see
398  W:   =communicated I I wouldn't speak to him
399        because I just hated him so very much
400        (.hhhhh) =
401       [          ]
402  T:   [right, ((nods yes)) you were so angr]
403  W:   =and he would just come over, I work three
404        days a week and he would come over and
405        take my son and (.hhh) in the afternoon,
```

```
406        >and then I he would bring him back in the
407        morning ((therapist nods yes)) and I usu-
408        ally would only see him when he dropped
409        him off and he would walk in and I would
410        hand him his over night bag and and say
411        >see you later< ((therapist nods yes)) and
412        that would be it we never socialized we
413        never talked<
414            [
415  T:         [((therapist crosses legs, similar
416        to wife's posture)) Right (.1) and so, and
417        so what, I'm a little mystified given that
418        (.hhh) (.4) lately you've been communicat
419        ing more, and (ah:?)=
```

After getting the wife's response of "New York, *yeah*" (line 370), O'Hanlon pursues his earlier agenda by first repeating "that that kind of thing" (lines 372–373) was nice. "That kind of thing" refers to the trip to New York. O'Hanlon repeats that the trip was "nice" in order to highlight this point and get an agreement from both the husband and wife. The husband acknowledges this statement with a head nod (line 376), while the wife at first does not acknowledge his statement (line 377).

After an audible breath intake, O'Hanlon then adds "and it sorta got washed out for you by the knowledge she was there in the background" (lines 377–380). The breath intake allowed O'Hanlon to evaluate his assertion and see what more he might need to add in order for his statement to be accepted by the wife. He then modifies his assertion by adding "and it sort of got washed out for you" (lines 377–378). This acknowledges the wife's previous turns. The wife nods yes to this modification.

O'Hanlon further modifies his comment by adding "his energy was still there in some ways" (lines 380–381). This (re)formulation of the wife's turn (lines 355–362) both accepts the wife's assertions while also modifying them via diluting the wife's critical comments ("his car was parked right there") into a softer form ("his energy was there in some ways"). This allows for O'Hanlon to soften the assumptions of the wife's rejection assertions, in order to lead the conversation back to his original agenda.

O'Hanlon then returns to his earlier question, ten turns previous (lines 304–321), pursuing an answer regarding good times that they had had together. The wife however, again does not give the answer that O'Hanlon is seeking. As the wife says, "Not really because we really didn't (line 392), O'Hanlon overlaps her turn. The wife, however, continues her turn as she explains why she cannot give an answer to his question. During this stretch of talk, the therapist overlaps the wife's turns four times. The wife pursues

her agenda until the fourth time (line 415), when the therapist achieves a
complete turn, as seen in the beginning of the following segment.

```
415  T:        [((therapist crosses legs, similar
416        to wife's posture)) Right (.1) and so, and
417        so what, I'm a little mystified given that
418        (.hhh) (.4) lately you've been communicat-
419        ing more, and (ah:?)=
420  W:    =Well we just moved in together.
421  T:    OK you moved back together=
422                  [
423  W:                  [yes ((husband and
424        wife both nod yes))
425  T:    =what got you to make that decision >I
426        mean< <I just want to ask> ((wife puts her
427        hands to her hair and shakes her head no))
428        (you may be thinking)=
429  W:    =((laughter) (   )
430  T:    ((therapist puts his hands to his head))
431        ((husband looks at wife and then husband
432        laughs)) NOBODY COULD GET ME TO MAKE THAT
433        DECISION WHY:::? was I so:: cra:zy? (.hhh)
434        but (.2) why I mean ((wife crosses arms
435        over chest)) wh what got you to make you
436        certainly wanned it you decided this is
437        the direction I want to go in ((husband
438        nods yes)) and I have the choice to go
439        another way:: but (.hhh) given everything
440        that's happened given the background given
441        what the: relationship between you two you
442        say "I want this" (.hh) and you s: before
443        you before you used to just hand him his
444        bag and off he went and you know:: ((wife
445        nods yes)) (trapped, kicked or whatever)
446              [                        ]
447  W:          [Well: the thing that did] it
448        to me is his girlfriend called me up and
449        she said "Carrie is it true that you're
450        going back with him" and and at this point
451        I I had not made the decision and I said
452        (.hhh) "He keeps calling me he keeps writ-
453        ing me letters and and begging me to come
454        back, but I can't, I ((therapist nods
455        yes)) can't live with someone that could
456        hate me so much to do this to me (.hhh)
```

```
457        And I sez I just can't have anything to do
458        with it (.hhh)
459          [
460   T:    [Ri:ght ((nods yes))
461   W:    Well, he kept trying, he kept trying, and I
462        knew that he was not making any contact
463        with her because she kept calling me on a
464        daily basis saying = ((therapist nods yes))
465   T:    = Trying to find out what his story was (.1)
466        ok? ((nods yes))
467                                           [
468   W:                                      [yeah,
469        yeah ((unfolds arms)) and so so ah she
470        said "he called me and said he wouldn't
471        have anything to do with me and that it
472        was over with between us." And so I knew
473        this and obviously he had proven to me
474        (.hhh) that finally he was possibly gonna
475        drop her. =
```

In his turn, beginning on line 415, O'Hanlon poses a question in order to clarify an unclear reference by the wife. In asking, "I'm a little mystified given that (.hhh) (.4) lately you've been communicating more" (lines 417–419), O'Hanlon is using an ambiguous reference to find out why they are in the therapy session together. He is assuming that since they are together in the session, they must have some motivating reasons for resolving their relationship. Since the wife has only been offering reasons of why she does not want to be with her husband, O'Hanlon's question is seeking clarification from the wife on what has led her to want to resolve their problems. His question is therefore designed to elicit information from the wife that will assist him in pursuing examples of solution-oriented behaviors.

The interpretation that the wife gives to O'Hanlon's question can be seen in her response, "Well we just moved in together" (line 421). Her understanding of the question is to explain why they are not communicating well. The clarifying information conveyed in her response focuses on time. Since they just recently moved back together, there has not been enough time to have experienced any good communication.

O'Hanlon, in pursuit of a different answer from the wife uses the combination of humor and posing a question and then answering it himself to change the topic of her assertion and to get her to focus on a solution-oriented behavior. O'Hanlon poses the question to the wife, "what got you to make that decision" (line 425). The wife laughs at O'Hanlon's exaggerated body movements and his emphasis on the word "what." O'Hanlon continues with his turn while the wife is laughing, and before she can respond to his question.

He further exaggerates the wife's position as he states, "NOBODY COULD GET ME TO MAKE THAT DECISION WHY:::? was I so:: cra:zy?" (lines 432–433). He then repeats the question, "wh what got you to make" (line 435) and before he finishes the question, he offers an answer himself. O'Hanlon states, "you certainly wanned it you decided this is the direction I want to go in" (lines 435–437) and then he speaks for the wife. He states, "I have the choice to go another way:: but (.hhh) given every-thing . . . you say 'I want this' " (lines 438–442). In this sequence O'Hanlon is supplying his own answers for the wife. There must be some real reason as to why she chose to go back to her husband.

This procedure finally works. The wife answers the therapist's question with an example of something good that has happened for the two of them. She tells the therapist the reason she moved back and believed her hus-band's sincerity was because the girlfriend was calling her (lines 461–475). O'Hanlon finally elicits the type of answer that he has pursued for 23 turns.

Summary

To review the above discussion, O'Hanlon used a variety of procedures to pursue a particular response from the wife. He pursued a response over many turns. He offered candidate answers to elicit a particular response. He would overlap his talk with the wife's turns in order to get his turn. He would seek to clarify the wife's understanding of the facts, and he would (re)formulate new understandings of her assertions in order to develop a new shared understanding with the wife. He sought to clarify unclear refer-ences. He modified his assertions until he was able to elicit the desired response from the wife. O'Hanlon posed questions to the wife, and before she could answer them, he would supply the answer that would lead to the response he was seeking. Finally, he used humor to change the topic from a problematic issue towards the topic he was pursuing.

These extended segments were used to demonstrate the different proce-dures used by O'Hanlon in his pursuit of a class of solution-oriented re-sponses throughout the session. Through these procedures, O'Hanlon was continuously sensitive to the interactional comments of the husband and wife. He would calibrate and modify his talk, via these nine procedures, in order to create a tightly woven therapy tapestry. These procedures allowed him to cut (interrupt) strands of talk that would drift away from the pattern he was cocreating and to restitch other strands of talk back into the pattern.

Chapter 5
Discussion

This project has brought the research methods of ethnomethodology and conversation analysis to the family therapy field. In a review of family therapy process research literature, it has been shown that there is a need for new methodologies that are capable of fully studying the family therapy paradigm. Ethnomethodology and conversation analysis were described as an approach to fill this gap. In order to demonstrate the utility of the conversation analytic approach, and in order to examine more carefully the therapeutic processes of solution-oriented therapy, the work of William O'Hanlon was selected.

A one-session consultation session by O'Hanlon was videotaped, audiotaped, and then transcribed. The transcript was then analyzed following the procedures of conversation analysis. Through this analysis, an understanding of the interactive patterns of the therapist/couple system was developed. In addition, this analysis described O'Hanlon's therapeutic procedures for pursuing particular types of responses from the clients.

Contributions to Solution-oriented Therapy

This study has examined the process of change in the one-session consultation case of William O'Hanlon. Meeting the recommendations of Weakland (1987) to analyze an entire session, this project carefully explored the therapeutic procedures used by O'Hanlon. O'Hanlon has previously articulated his approach towards solution-oriented therapy and described the therapeutic interventions used in this approach (O'Hanlon & Wilk, 1987; O'Hanlon & Weiner-Davis, 1989). While O'Hanlon does demonstrate a fit between his theory of change and what he actually does in therapy, examining the marital session generated additional descriptions and understandings of his skills.

One result gained from analyzing the text was an understanding of his unarticulated procedures for pursuing particular types of responses. These procedures are a class of interventions designed to deal with problematic behaviors by specifically pursuing a class of responses from the clients. As noted earlier, O'Hanlon and Wilk (1987) advocated developing new and "updated descriptive generalizations for identifying what it is we do"

(p. 111). In this conversation analysis of the marital session, a set of procedures was described that presented, in detail, how the therapist pursues a class of solution-oriented responses from his clients. The nine procedures share some features of O'Hanlon and Wilk's (1987) and O'Hanlon and Weiner-Davis' (1989) descriptions, but they also add some completely new descriptions.

These therapeutic procedures, adapted from Pomerantz' (1987, 1988) work, provide a classification of how O'Hanlon pursues a class of solution-oriented responses. These procedures are used when the clients are either not agreeing with the therapeutic agenda, or they are offering responses contrary to the class of behaviors that the therapist is attempting to elicit. These interventions are designed to elicit a particular class of behaviors from the clients, that is, solution-oriented responses. In the session analyzed in this study, when the wife or husband would not respond with solution-oriented responses, the therapist would use these procedures to modify and change their responses towards a solution-oriented theme. Through changing their responses, O'Hanlon was eliciting new types of behaviors from the couple. Of these nine procedures, five have been previously described (O'Hanlon & Wilk, 1987; O'Hanlon & Weiner-Davis, 1989), while four of these interventions have not been previously described by O'Hanlon.

The four procedures not previously described include O'Hanlon's pursuing a response over many turns, clarifying unclear references and modifying his assertions. In addition, another procedure used by O'Hanlon, and not previously described, is his procedure of posing questions to the clients as well as answering these questions as if he were speaking for the client.

Of the five procedures previously described, offering a candidate answer is similar to asking multiple choice questions. It is different in that offering a candidate answer serves the purpose of both eliciting particular responses as well as presenting how well the therapist understands the clients' previous assertions. Simply providing possible answers that are too far afield from the client's stated views would not be effective.

The therapist overlapping his talk with the husband's or wife's turn is similar to therapeutic interruptions, but highlights how O'Hanlon's overlapping turns are designed to provide him with a turn and can persist over many turns. Through carefully not completing the overlap until the other speaker relinquished his/her turn, the therapist would continue to overlap until the other speaker ceased his/her turn and the therapist could continue with his turn at speaking.

(Re)formulation is comparable to summary with a twist, and offers more descriptive details of how O'Hanlon uses this strategy in a session. The use of humor to change a topic from a problematic description to a non-problem perspective is similar to O'Hanlon and Wilk's (1987) use of humor, but differs in that it is specifically used to disrupt the client's talk as well as change the focus of the conversation.

Ignoring the client's misunderstandings or assertions is similar to O'Hanlon and Wilk's (1987) strategy of deliberately ignoring certain communications of the client. This pursuit procedure operates in a similar manner in that through ignoring the client's response, it "presupposes that a particular matter is not worth discussing or is not relevant to the solution of a problem" (p. 84). As one of the pursuit procedures, this intervention is used to ignore rival classes of responses by the clients.

Through the conversation analytic approach, a clearer and more detailed understanding of the therapeutic process can be discerned. These nine interventions are sophisticated rhetorical devices that are effective in shifting the conversation to following a particular pattern. If they are not performed well, these procedures could result in ending a conversation prematurely. For example, if through overlapping his talk with the client's turn at talking, the therapist were to continue talking as the client continued talking, this could be construed as a rude act. If this continued many times, the client might be offended and feel no rapport with the therapist. O'Hanlon, while he would pursue his turn through many overlap approaches, would not continue his turn at speaking until the other speaker relinquished his/her turn (via pausing).

If the therapist (re)formulates the client's talk without any regard for what the client had said previously, the client may again feel at odds with the therapist. As the therapist speaks for the clients, answering the very questions he poses to them, it is again crucial that O'Hanlon respond in a manner that is not too far from the realm of possible responses that the client him/herself might utter. In offering (re)formulations of the clients' assertions, O'Hanlon would also include paraphrases of statements they had actually made. Through telling stories and leaving ambiguous whether he is speaking for characters of the story, or for the husband and wife in the session, O'Hanlon is able to speak for the clients, crediting new types of assertions to the clients, in a nonobtrusive manner.

These nine techniques of pursuit, in addition to representing a class of interventions used by O'Hanlon, also demonstrate the conversational nature of therapy. As Szasz (1978) pointed out, seeing therapy as a conversation requires that "we must look anew at the subject of rhetoric and assess its relevance to mental healing" (p. 11). The analysis of this session, and the demonstration of these procedures, highlight Szasz' comments and emphasize the importance of examining language in the therapeutic setting, as opposed to "the error of classifying [therapy] as a medical intervention" (Szasz, 1978, p. 11).

A further implication of this notion of therapy as conversation is the question as to whether O'Hanlon's therapeutic language is the same as "ordinary conversation" which differs from everyday talk only in terms of the "goal in conducting [the] conversation" (O'Hanlon & Wilk, 1987, p. 177). Are these rhetorical devices used by O'Hanlon features of conversations used in nontherapeutic settings? Are the rhetorical devices used by other change agents (sales personal, lawyers, counselors, etc.) different or similar to these procedures for pursuing a class of responses? Further research in this area would reveal important information regarding this topic.

These nine interventions also provide a method for O'Hanlon to calibrate the degree to which the clients were changing their view of the problem. As Pinsof (1988) and Safran et al. (1988) have noted, recognizing small-o outcome changes within the therapy session helps to provide greater detailed understanding of the therapy process. Changes in the client's responses achieved by these pursuit strategies would be an indicator that small-o outcome changes, or a moment of change, have/has occurred.

While the nine therapeutic procedures to pursue a class of responses are not meant to represent the only factors involved in the solution-oriented therapeutic process, they do represent a description of the way in which O'Hanlon worked in this one session consultation. This analysis reveals the multifaceted procedures and determination of the therapist as he pursues a particular agenda in the session. The analysis also reveals how the clients and therapist together create an interactive system and how each participant's agenda contributes to the construction of that system. In addition, the analysis reveals how O'Hanlon must modify his talk in order to accommodate the other members of the system, and pursue, via therapeutic strategies, alterations in the structure and pattern of that system.

It should also be noted that in pursuit of his solution-oriented agenda, O'Hanlon would often refer back to assertions made many turns earlier. This is in contrast to replies made to the client's statement in the turn just prior to the therapist's turn. This type of response, referring to elements of a conversation mentioned many turns earlier (Goffman, 1981), may reflect another unique characteristic of O'Hanlon's work. More research on this topic would be useful.

Contributions of Conversation Analysis to the Family Therapy Field

The need for new research methodologies in family therapy has been cited by many researchers (Gurman, 1988; Pinsof, 1988; Reiss, 1988; Steier, 1988; Wynne, 1988c) in order to analyze the unique aspects of the family therapy paradigm. Methodologies have been sought that are contextually sensitive (Greenberg, 1986a, 1986b; Gurman et al., 1986), able to examine the actions of both the therapist and the clients (Gurman et al., 1986; Small & Manthei, 1986), incorporate systemic and cybernetic concepts (Auerswald, 1988; Keeney, 1982; Stanton, 1988), develop behaviorally focused microtheory (Rice & Greenberg, 1984; Pinsof, 1986) and provide clinicians with information relevant to their practices (Andreozzi, 1985; Luborsky, 1972; Orlinsky & Howard, 1978; Steier, 1988).

Many of the new methodologies in the family therapy field (Greenberg, 1984, 1986a, 1986b; Greenberg & Pinsof, 1986; Gurman et al., 1986; Pinsof, 1986; Rice & Greenberg, 1984a; Wynne, 1988a) have focused on discovery-oriented approaches to research. In the search to find those "moments of movements" (Mahrer, 1985), or how change occurs in the therapy session (Rogers, 1942), these new methodologies have been directed towards the "process" of therapy, rather than the "outcome" of therapy. However, many of these approaches have not been able to incorporate the features of preserving the contextual integrity of the session, examining the interactions of *both* therapist and client, considering systemic concepts, developing behaviorally focused microtheory and in addition, bear relevance to clinicians.

Conversation analysis is a methodology capable of yielding such a mixture of information. As seen in Chapter 4, conversation analysis preserves the contextual integrity of the session. This methodology also allows the reader to draw conclusions based on the exemplars and whether or not they validate the descriptions of the transcript. This feature helps resolve the difficulty of researcher/observer bias (Steier, 1988; Wynne, 1988c) as it makes plain to the reader how the researcher is making sense of the data.

The conversation analytical approach used here also looked at the behaviors of *both* the clients *and* the therapist. In weaving their performative conversations together, the analysis was able to consider the triadic system formed during the session, as well as view the reflexive response of each participant. Such a perspective allows a better systemic understanding of the therapeutic process, including: (a) how problems are constructed and defined through interactions, (b) how each person influences the other in a circular or recursive manner, that is, incorporating the concept of feedback, (c) how the therapist (and each client) strives to direct the system in a particular direction (d) how the therapist constantly modifies his interventions and strategies in order to accommodate problematic issues.

Through the interactions of the three participants of the therapy system, it could be observed how each would impact the conversation towards co-creating meanings of the others' behaviors. The wife would paint one picture of the husband, while O'Hanlon would try to describe another understanding of the husband's behavior. The husband, through his actions to maintain a neutral position, would not disagree with either the wife or therapist, as he strived to appease his wife. Each participant's actions and statements were recursively influenced by the responses of the other two members, as the system was continuously shifting in meaning. In this manner the participants both cocreated the triadic system as simultaneously the triadic system influenced their actions. The conversation is therefore both context-shaped and context-renewing.

Conversation analysis applied here is useful in helping to expand behaviorally focused micro theory as it examines, in detail, "change episodes" (Gurman et al, 1986). The descriptions and understanding of "how" O'Hanlon would pursue particular responses from the clients are at a micro, change episode level. Such descriptions help understand solution focused therapy by fleshing out additional procedures used by O'Hanlon to accomplish his stated goals. In addition, these descriptions offer clinicians specific procedures to follow in the pursuit of responses in sessions.

Conversation analysis is an approach that incorporates many aspects of other methodologies. It is capable of duplicating task analysis procedures (Rice & Greenberg, 1984b) in the naturalistic setting of the therapy session as well as including the therapist's actions in the process. This approach incorporates both paralinguistic features (Rice & Kerr, 1986; Scheflen, 1973) as well as kinesic features (Scheflen, 1973) of the session. Conversation analysis also provides a methodology for examining "moments of movement" (Mahrer, 1985) as it tracks the process of therapy.

Conversation analysis examines change through the language of the participants and not simply from the perspective of the therapist's description of what he/she proposes to do in therapy. The language of change and the language of analysis become the ordinary language used by all clients. This approach provides a method to examine: (a) the fit between the therapist's theory of change with what he/she actually does in therapy; (b) the various manners in which clients change during the therapeutic process ("small-o outcome," Safran et al., 1988); (c) the comparison of different approaches to therapy with each other.

This study extends the work done by Lennard and Bernstein (1960). In their seminal work, they noted that clients, over time, tend to speak in a similar manner as their therapist. Through content analysis, they examined how the client's vocabulary changed over the course of therapy and became similar to the therapist's vocabulary. This investigation points out that not only is the content of the client's words relevant, but *how* he/she communicates is crucial.

In the session analyzed, when the wife joked about being "paranoid," laughed at her own negativity, and how she was the one who would often introduce the girlfriend into conversations, she was reflecting the solution-oriented manner of the therapist. This new class of behaviors by the client can be observed only by examining the context of the conversation. The clients are not simply learning a new language with which to communicate, but they are learning a new way of interacting.

Evaluating the client's actions. This approach to analysis provides a method for evaluating the client's action. Often, in reviews or analyses of therapy sessions, the clients are examined from the perspective of the therapist. How the therapist understands the clients' issues and system becomes the reader's understanding of the clients' system. Conversation analysis allows the reader to view the system through the actions of each participant. How each participant is achieving a particular result can be described. In the session analyzed in this study, both the wife's and husband's actions and agenda were analyzed. Indeed, it could be seen how effective the wife was in pursuing her own agenda towards placing blame upon the husband. It is precisely because the wife was so persistent in her pursuits, that it required O'Hanlon to doggedly pursue his agenda of eliciting solution-oriented responses.

Application to clinicians. This project, while examining the work of a solution-focused therapist, can also be applied to other schools of family therapy. Regardless of the language of change described by a particular orientation of family therapy, conversation analysis examines how change occurs in the session using the language of the participants. A difficulty of current process research is "establishing agreement on how to describe therapy in general terms in the face of the . . . various specific theories" (Small & Manthei, 1986, p. 395).

. While O'Hanlon was pursuing a specific class of responses, each school of therapy will also pursue a particular class of responses. The procedures of pursuit are applicable to any of the orientations of family therapy as they provide a detailed description of how to elicit responses from the clients. While not every weaver will create the same tapestry, the nine procedures of pursuing a response do provide therapists of different orientations with the cross stitches from which to construct a tightly crafted tapestry.

The methodology of this study also reveals the importance of the clinician's communication in the therapy session. While not claiming to represent all elements of the therapy process, this project does focus on the therapeutic conversation. This study provides clinicians with a method with which to view their own clinical work to determine when their interventions are effective. Through viewing how the client and therapist communicate, the clinician can assess those instances when interventions are not taking. Through subtle differences in communication patterns, powerful changes can be elicited by the clinician. In addition to viewing their own clinical work, modifications of this methodology also offer possibilities for use in supervision and training of other family therapists.

Limitations

It is important to state that the procedures of pursuit used by O'Hanlon are not meant to represent all of his interventions. They are, however, one important class of interventions which he uses in the session. This study only examined some elements of the therapy session; to be all-encompassing would be impossible.

This investigation analyzed a one-session consultation demonstration by William O'Hanlon. He (personal communication) described this session as highly representative of his therapy style. In his writings (O'Hanlon & Wilk, 1987; O'Hanlon & Weiner-Davis, 1989), he describes frequently using this approach with clients for only one session. Questions of generalizability to solution-oriented therapy can be raised. However, through building up a corpus of solution-oriented therapy conversations, the degree to which this session is representative of solution-oriented therapy can be established.

O'Hanlon is recognized as a master instructor in the family therapy field, and as such, is a leader in developing new ideas and interventions. The procedures of pursuit described in this study, while pertaining to solution-oriented therapy, reflect the class of procedures for pursuing responses in any therapeutic setting. For these reasons, these procedures are applicable to family therapists in general.

Recommendations

This study yields many possible questions for further research. What other classes of interventions does O'Hanlon employ in his therapy? How does this session compare to other solution-oriented sessions with O'Hanlon as the therapist? Does he work differently when the case lasts more than one session? What procedures do clients follow in therapy? Do clients pursue different agendas for different types of therapy? Do clients pursue different agendas when seen individually as opposed to marital/family therapy? In addition, this methodology could be used to compare how different family therapists, from different schools of family therapy, pursue their therapeutic agenda. The relationship of how clients' view what they see as important in therapy (Elliott, 1986) following the session, can be compared with *how* they respond during the session.

From this study, it is possible to see the powerful effect language can have in impacting the behavior of people. Through the use of rhetorical devices, the therapeutic conversation functions to weave for clients new constructions of their social reality. As Davis (1984) points out in her paper, (re)formulation can be used in a way to constrain and hinder the client. In a like manner, the approaches used by O'Hanlon, and therapists in general, can have a strong impact on how clients choose to construct their reality. For this reason, it is urged that the reader use their rhetorical skills wisely, in a respectful and caring manner.

Appendix A
Transcript Notation

(.)	A pause which is noticeable but too short to measure.
(.5)	A pause timed in tenths of a second.
=	There is no discernable pause between the end of a speaker's utterance and the start of the next utterance.
:	One or more colons indicate an extension of the preceding vowel sound.
<u>Under</u>	Underlining indicates words that were uttered with added emphasis.
CAPITAL	Words in capitals are uttered louder than the surrounding talk.
(.hhh)	Exhale of breath.
(hhh)	Inhale of breath.
( )	Material in parentheses are inaudible or there is doubt of accuracy.
[	Overlap of talk.
(( ))	Double parentheses indicate clarificatory information, e.g., ((laughter)).
?	Indicates a rising inflection.
!	Indicates an animated tone.
.	Indicates a stopping fall in tone.
* *	Talk between * * is quieter than surrounding talk.
> <	Talk between > < is said quicker than surrounding talk.

Transcript of O'Hanlon Session

((Wife sits with her legs crossed, husband sits next to her with his legs apart, resting on the floor, and the therapist sits with his feet both on the floor, close together))

01 *T:*   So what I need to know is (.2)
02   esse:ntially: what either:: brought chew
03   for help initially: for counselling or
04   whatever it may be if (hh) you if you've
05   done I've I specifically asked (.hhh) not
06   to know anything about what >your situa-
07   tion is so I can< come with a fresh vie::w
08   and (.hhh) giveye some fresh ideas hope-
09   fully(:) and >help you move along to where
10   ever you want to go:(.hhh)< ((wife and
11   husband nod yes)) a:n: that's: what I need
12   to know, is (.hh) either what brings ya
13   toda::::y whh: and more than that maybe to
14   help me orient to where we are suppos::ed
15   to go where you hope to go (.hhh) ho:w
16   will you know ((swallowed)) if we've done
17   wonderful things here ((wife nods yes)) an
18   everything is worked out and you gotten
19   what you came for (.hh) and your relation-
20   ship for each other ah whatever it may be
21   how will you know when actually (.) things
22   are better (.hh) and ah or things are
23   where you want them to be in your rela-
24   tionship or whatever you've come for. So,
25   (.hh) I want to ask each of you >how will
26   I know< and then I may ask you some ques-
27   tions >so I make sure I understand that<
28   >in a pretty good way< (.hh) and I want to
29   know how you'll know ultimately and what
30   will be the first sign to see (.) things
31   are going in a good direction, so (.) from
32   either of you, whoever wants to start.
33   ((looks at both husband and wife))
34 *H:*   ((looks towards wife)) You made the call you
35   could (.8) you want to talk first?

```
36              [
37  W:          [((laughter)) ((wife sits with legs
38          crossed))
39  T:      Alright so you made the call and we'll put
40              it on her first OK= ((therapist crosses
41              legs))
42  W:      ((laughing)) =Oh good, um (clear throat
43              twice) basically we we'll be married
44          tomorrow will be our eighth year anniver-
45          sery=
46  T:          =Uh huh=
47  W:      =and ah
48              [
49  T:          [congratulations= ((crosses legs simi-
50              larly to wife's position))
51  W:      (.hh) =we have a two year old (two) son
52              (.h) with a two year old son ahm (.hh)
53              we've had (hhh) a troubled marriage I
54              think I would say the first three years
55              were happy ((therapist nods yes)) and
56              after that we we kinda just (.hh) we went
57              to counseling a couple of other times
58              ((therapist nods yes)) either I was
59              unhappy or he was unhappy (.hhh) and with
60              the counseling ourselves or were whatever
61              ((therapist nods yes)) with the person
62              that we were with (.hhh) but ahm (cleared
63              throat) (.3) we really (.hh) (.4) we just
64              (hhh) (.4) I ah I think what we've agreed
65              upon is that (.hh) when we when we set
66              goals we have an easier time reaching them
67              but when we don't have anything to work
68              towards I mean like >I put him through
69              school ((therapist nods yes)) I worked two
70              jobs putting him through school< (.hhh)
71              and I just (.hhh) we we moved to New Mexico
72              at one point in our marriage about a year
73              after we were married >but we saved and we
74              worked to get to that it seems like if we
75              have a goal to reach then we work
76              together fine:: but< (.hhh) like since
77              when our son was born we are kinda laying
78              in limbo and we really haven't (.hhh)=
79  T:          =right= ((nods head yes))
80  W:      =I don't know and our our most important
81              thing is communication we haven't had any
82              (.hh) we just miss each other like I'll
```

83		meet him and I'll say something's wrong
84		and he'll say "no nothing's wrong, noth-
85		ing's wrong" ((therapist nods yes)) and
86		that's what led up to this point recently
87		(hhh) >March 13 I'll never forget the
88		date< ((therapist nods yes)) (brief laugh)
89		(.hhh) he had been (.hh) ahm coming home
90		late from work (1.0) ((therapist nods
91		yes)) ((swallows and turns towards hus-
92		band)) and I'm not saying this to hurt you
93		just to help us (.hhh) so he had been=
94		[
95	H:	[I know *I know*
96	W:	=coming home late from work and he just was
97		didn't (.) didn't care he wasn't there I
98		just could see it in his eyes: ((therapist
99		nods yes)) (.hhh) well he came home March
100		13 and announced that he was seeing
101		somebody ((therapist nods yes)) (.hh) and
102		that (.hh) he thought possibly, >she was a
103		very good friend< and I could see that he
104		was falling in love with her well she
105		called our house (.hhh) I stayed living
106		(.) there for about two months (hhh) no
107		about a month and a half (.hhh) and she
108		called our house like three times a day
109		((therapist nods yes)) and she would talk
110		to him and they would giggle like girl-
111		friend and boyfriend and everything and
112		this mean (.hh) meanwhile was eating away
113		at me inside ((therapist nods yes)) and my
114		heart was was breaking (.hhh) well it
115		reached to the point where we couldn't
116		live together and I I just wanted to stay
117		there cause I was on a maid shift I didn't
118		have anyone to watch my son ((therapist
119		nods yes)) and so (.hhh) about a a month
120		and half later after this had all (hhh)
121		been established and I knew there was a
122		relationship with my husband (.hhh) with
123		another girl then I moved into my mother's
124		house ((therapist nods yes)) and which
125		was extremely stressful (.hhh) ahm::
126		(1.0 pause)
127	T:	But you had somebody to watch the two year
128		old, ((wife nods yes)) so that that sort
129		of handled that. =

```
130                                    [
131  W:                              [Yeah  = yeah my
132         sister took over and watched while I slept
133         for four hours in the morning and ((ther-
134         apist nods yes)) (.hhh) I wasn't sleeping
135         at this point I couldn't sleep hardly at
136         all =
137  T:   = Because of the emotional upsets and all
138         that.
139  W:   So, um, but I have lost 56 pounds? ((laugh-
140         ter)) since March ((laughter)).
141  T:   That's good? that isn't ba:d? ((gestures to
142         the left and right, smiles, husband looks
143         at therapist and then husband smiles))
144  W:   I got one good thing I have my figure back =
145         ((laughs)).
146                 [                        ]
147  T:           [Some people would say]
148  T:   = Say maybe you can write a new diet book,
149         the ah, husband having an affair diet
150         book, it's not (.9) no maybe for every-
151         body? but
152                                       [
153  W:                                  [((laughs
154         and nods head yes)) Yep, yep so anyway at
155         this point I I did seek counseling ahm
156         through I work, I am a nurse at (name)
157         Medical Center (.hhh) and I I went there
158         and they said you know at this point you
159         have a lot on your mind you're going
160         through a lot of emotional stress (.hhh)
161         ((therapist nods yes)) and they said you
162         are in what we consider a a depression
163         ((therapist nods yes)) and I couldn't eat
164         I remember at one point I didn't (.hhh) I
165         would'nt starving myself I just didn't
166         realize I was hungry
167                        [
168  T:                  [yeah. ((shrugs his should-
169         ders))
170  W:   I couldn't sleep, I couldn't eat I I hadn't
171         eaten anything for probably 13 ((therapist
172         nods yes)) days so she re (.hh) told me to
173         go and see this psychiatrist and I saw
174         (name) on Fifth Street for ahh (.hh) maybe
175         four or five visits I couldn't (.hhh) I
176         didn't get anything from her I needed
```

```
177          someone to wake me up to life and just say
178          you know >this is where you are at this is
179          what you have to do these are your goals<
180          ((therapist nods yes)) and and she just
181          kinda said "how do you feel about that?"
182          and "what are you doing?" ((therapist nods
183          yes)) and and you know an an it just it
184          didn't get me to where I wanted to go, I
185          needed someone to shake me and be alive
186          again=
187                                    [
188  T:                               [*right* ((ther-
189          apist nods yes))
190  W:   =I don't know (.hhh) so I stopped going to
191          her ((swallowed)) ahm, (.5) (.hhh) so:
192          his:: affair went on it's been eight long
193          months that have hard on both of us and
194          (.hh)=
195                                [
196  T:                           [*right*
197  W:   =I think um (.5) there was a lot of lies a
198          lot of lot of just hateful things that
199          were done (.hhh) ((therapist nods yes))
200          and (.) he kinda pleads temporary insanity
201          which I think is a very poor excuse
202          ((therapist nods yes and no)) and I find
203          that hard to forgive him for that and=
204                                       [
205  T:                                  [*right*
206  W:   =(.hhh) it's I don't think it's fair that I
207          should be be asked to just forgive him and
208          pretend like that's temporary insanity
209          ((therapist nods yes)) I don't you know
210          think that's asking a lot from me (.hhh)=
211          (hhhhh)
212                [                      ]
213  T:   =And he says [look at (all) you know] this
214          is craziness I went through now its so::
215          it on tha:t (.5) (.) Is it done?
216          ((therapist leans forward and looks at
217          husband as he says this, uncrosses legs
218          and sits similarly to the husband's posi-
219          tion))
220  H:   ((nodding yes)) I want it to be done, yes.
221  T:   ((therapist looks at both the husband and
222          wife)) Ok I mean is the but is the contact
```

223		with this person::: ah in the <u>past</u> or is
224		that still going on?
225	*H:*	That's ahh ((looks up and to his right))
226		(.hhh) (1.0) I would say it's ah <u>95</u> per-
227		cent over (.) ((therapist nods yes)) she
228		tries to contact me at work =
229	*T:*	= Ok, so from your side you said ok I want to
230		put this thing back together ((wife and
231		husband nod yes)) do what I can to put it
232		back together (.hh) ((husband nods yes))
233		she still sometimes tries to ahm get some
234		contact with ((husband nods yes)) you as
235		much as possible you (.8) (.hh) you've
236		been shoving it to the side ((gestures to
237		the right)) ((husband nods yes)).
238	*W:*	She's called me whenever she
239		[
240	*T:*	[Right ((nodding
241		yes)) She also contacted you so that (.2)
242		occasionally stirs things up ((husband
243		nods yes))
244		[
245	*W:*	[*yep*
246	*T:*	but for the most part (.) th (.hh) I
247		assume the reason you two are here
248		together is you're saying ok: if it's pos-
249		sible to put this thing back together (.)
250		to get ((wife nods yes)) (.) to some good
251		place (husband nods yes)) that's what we
252		would like to do we would like to (.hh)
253		get the affair behind us and get back
254		((wife nods yes)) to:: (.hh) <u>some</u> of
255		things that we used to do ((husband nods
256		yes)) that were good like the first three
257		years as you said that were <u>happier,</u>
258		closer, less conflict (.hh) and be able to
259		lea::ve this one behind and say <u>how</u> can I
260		(.) somehow let go of this ((wife nods
261		yes)) and work through it ((husband nods
262		yes)) or forgive (.) or forget or (.hh) if
263		not forgive and forget somehow put this
264		(.hh) in its place so that we <u>can</u>: move on
265		and build something else (.2) So ok
266		((therapist leans back in his chair))
267		(.hh) thats what you're after now and it's
268		somehow (.hh) f:ind out whether it is sort

```
269          of like skate or get off the ic:e pond
270          ((wife nods yes)) but for the most part
271          because you showed up togeth together
272          you're thinking it's time to skate and
273          lets get on with this but we just (.) at
274          this point >don't know how::?<= ((wife and
275          husband both nod yes))
276              [        ]
277  W:          [*uh huh* ]
278  T:   = or we would like to know how: (.hh) to put
279          it back together. ((husband nods yes)) Ok.
280          (.hh) So: you know in in some ways you'd
281          you'd like to say "uh uh, >I don't want to
282          hear it anymore<, I mean I think I paid my
283          dues: ((therapist puts hands over his
284          ears)) fo:r you know all: of the things
285          that I did and I (.hh) I admit: >I was
286          wrong and it was crazy and all this stuff<
287          ((husband nods yes)) but now lets move on"
288          and you're saying, (.hhh) ">I don't find
289          it so easy just to let go of it and I
290          still get upset about it and I still need
291          to talk about it ((wife nods yes)) or or
292          whatever it may be<" (.hh) so ok, here we
293          are. (cough) Alright, so (1.0) in a
294          strange way, I wanna I wanna ask about
295          something that maybe other people didn't
296          ask about maybe they did ((wife nods yes))
297          (.hhh) (.) that is *what I'd like to know
298          is* te:ll me about (1.2) I guess
299          first what I would like to know is: Times
300          in the las:t eight months in the midst of
301          all: the chaos and weird things ((wife
302          nods yes)) that have been happening (.hhh)
303          tell me about any times (.) that actually
304          things: *went ok like you either had
305          ((therapist counts on fingers)) a really
306          good discussion your communication was:
307          good* umm and or (.2) you know, th times
308          (1.0) when things were jus:t (1.1) better
309          for some inexplicable reason can you
310          remember a moment in there, an evening,
311          ah: day, (.hh) when actually (.2) the two
312          of you felt like (.1) *wow you know* >for
313          some reason we didn't have a conflict or
314          we had a conflict and we worked it out
315          very satisfactorily for both of us< (.hhh)
```

```
316              or we just had one of these pleasant
317              interactions that was really good, ca tell
318              me about one of those times cause I'm
319              going to try and ah (.hh) er find in there
320              some pieces that we can use to maybe (.1)
321              ah build something else for the future.
322   H:    Like we went to ah (name) park (.4) ((wife
323              nods yes)) with our son during the middle
324              of that (.9) and I thought it was a won-
325              derful day.
326   T:    Ok, would you agree that that was a pretty
327              good day?
328   W:    No, >because I knew she was still there.<=
329   T:    =Ok, so that
330                        [
331   W:    [>we spent the entire day together
332              and he kept saying I want this back
333              ((therapist nods yes)) I want my family
334              back and I am so sorry for all the hurt
335              I've done< ((therapist nods yes)) (.hhh)
336              and on the way home I said does she know
337              that you're with me today that we went on
338              this family daytrip, and he goes are you
339              going to call her and tell her, he was
340              scared to death I was going to call her
341              and tell her (.hhh) He did this (.) quite
342              a few times during our relationship where
343              he would say, (.hhh) >"God I want all this
344              back and I am so sorry I dropped it"<
345              (.hhh) but then I would sa
346                                        [
347   T:                            [But then other
348              things that he said made you sort ah think
349              is he rea:lly committed to
350                                        [
351   W:                            [Well she lives on
352              the sam:e (.1) >street as I do< and I=
353                                        [
354   T:                              [right
355   W:    =would like we would spend an evening
356              together at his parents' house and then I
357              would I would go home (.hh) and put my son
358              to sleep and he (.1) >I would call the
359              house and he was gone ((therapist nods
360              yes)) and I would call his work and he was
361              gone and I drove to her house and his car
362              was parked right there< (.hh) so
```

```
363                              [
364  T:                          [right, ok]  ((husband
365             shrugs shoulders)) So::, so but (.) that's
366             the ki:nd of thing you w::ould like to do
367             in the future you know like sp sp spend
368             like you just went ah where did go over
369             to, New York?
370  W:         New York, *yeah*. ((husband and wife both nod
371             yes))
372  T:         ((looks at husband)) And so that that kind
373             of thing is something you'd like to do
374             more of ((husband nods yes)) (.hh) those
375             family things: that: would be nic:e ((hus-
376             band nods yes)) and that was nice for you:
377             (.hh) ((looks at wife)) and it sort of got
378             washed out for you by the knowledge ((wife
379             nods yes)) that she was there in the back-
380             ground and he still was (.hh) his energy
381             was still there in some ways (.hhh) how
382             about then, then I need to ask you if
383             ((looks at husband)) maybe ask you some
384             more but (.8) (.hh) ((looks at wife)) any-
385             times that it was:: good in terms of what
386             you perceived (1.0) Any moments that were
387             good, even though you knew that that was
388             happening any moments or any evenings or
389             any days that you thought were good?
390             (.9     pause)
391  W:         ((Husband looks at wife to let her reply))
392             Not really because we really didn't =
393                     [
394  T:                 [ok
395  W:         = communicate and like the only time we =
396                     [
397  T:                 [I see
398  W:         = communicated I I wouldn't speak to him
399             because I just hated him so very much
400             (.hhh) =
401                 [        ]
402  T:         [right, ((nods yes)) you were so angr]
403  W:         = and he would just come over, I work three
404             days a week and he would come over and
405             take my son and (.hhh) in the afternoon,
406             >and then I he would bring him back in the
407             morning ((therapist nods yes)) and I usu-
408             ally would only see him when he dropped
409             him off and he would walk in and I would
```

410   hand him his over night bag and and say
411   >see you later< ((therapist nods yes)) and
412   that would be it we never socialized we
413   never talked<
414   [
415 *T:*   [((therapist crosses legs, similar
416   to wife's posture)) Right (.1) and so, and
417   so what, I'm a little mystified given that
418   (.hhh) (.4) lately you've been communicat-
419   ing more, and (ah:?)=
420 *W:* =Well we just moved in together.
421 *T:* OK you moved back together=
422   [
423 *W:*   [yes   ((husband and
424   wife both nod yes))
425 *T:* =what got you to make that decision >I
426   mean< <I just want to ask> ((wife puts her
427   hands to her hair and shakes her head no))
428   (you may be thinking)=
429 *W:* =((laughter)) (   )
430 *T:* ((therapist puts his hands to his head))
431   ((husband looks at wife and then husband
432   laughs)) NOBODY COULD GET ME TO MAKE THAT
433   DECISION WHY:::? was I so:: cra:zy? (.hhh)
434   but (.2) why I mean ((wife crosses arms
435   over chest)) wh what got you to make you
436   certainly wanned it you decided this is
437   the direction I want to go in ((husband
438   nods yes)) and I have the choice to go
439   another way:: but (.hhh) given everything
440   that's happened given the background given
441   what the: relationship between you two you
442   say "I want this" (.hh) and you s: before
443   you before you used to just hand him his
444   bag and off he went and you know:: ((wife
445   nods yes)) (trapped, kicked or whatever)
446   [   ]
447 *W:*   [Well: the thing that did] it
448   to me is his girlfriend called me up and
449   she said "(Carrie) is it true that you're
450   going back with him" and and at this point
451   I I had not made the decision and I said
452   (.hhh) "He keeps calling me he keeps writ-
453   ing me letters and and begging me to come
454   back, but I can't, I ((therapist nods
455   yes)) can't live with someone that could
456   hate me so much to do this to me (.hhh)

457   And I sez I just can't have anything to do
458   with it (.hhh)
459   [
460   *T:*   [Ri:ght ((nods yes))
461   *W:*   Well, he kept trying, he kept trying, and I
462   knew that he was not making any contact
463   with her because she kept calling <u>me</u> on a
464   daily basis saying= ((therapist nods yes))
465   *T:*   =Trying to find out what his story was (.1)
466   ok? ((nods yes))
467   [
468   *W:*   [yeah,
469   yeah ((unfolds arms)) and so so ah she
470   said "he called me and said he wouldn't
471   have anything to do with me and that it
472   was over with between us." And so I knew
473   this and obviously he had proven to me
474   (.hhh) that <u>finally</u> he was possibly gonna
475   <u>drop</u> her. =
476   *T:*   =So you saw some action from him and <u>that's</u>
477   <u>what</u> you needed to see? ((wife nods yes))
478   [
479   *W:*   [ye:ah:?
480   *T:*   some commitment (.hh) some action from him,
481   saying OK (.hh) at least he's moving in
482   this direction saying he wants (.hh) you
483   know <u>he doesn't want that</u> and he's ((wife
484   nods yes)) ge getting that (1.3) tossing
485   that away ehh you know avoiding that (.hh)
486   and saying *OK* I Would like <u>this</u> and then
487   you had to really say "(.hhh) alright I
488   seen some action now:: can:: (.) I: (.)
489   possibly:: (.2) (.hh) think about: getting
490   back together" And you and at that point
491   you said "OK (.1) I'm willing to <u>try</u>"
492   ((wife nods yes)) (1.0) Ok, so you two
493   moved back together and now you just had
494   this trip to New York, yes=
495   *W:*   =We ((shaking head no)) didn't want to move
496   back together. I don't think <u>I</u> really
497   ((therapist nods yes)) wanted to move back
498   together this was kinda pressured (.hhh)
499   my family has totally disowned me, my sis-
500   ter called me up ((therapist nods yes)) >I
501   have four brothers and sisters< and (.hh)
502   my parents are divorced I've been living
503   with my mother which was a high stress=

```
504                         [                    ]
505  T:                     [Yeah, you said that was
506           high stress]
507  W:      = situation she's (.hh) like to discipline my
508           my son ((therapist nods yes)) and he I
509           mean we were always beaten as kids we
510           always we never (.hhh) I mean if we did
511           anything wrong my mom beat the hell out of
512           us ((therapist nods yes)) and we were sent
513           to our room and and I mean there was beat-
514           ing there wasn't just a smack
515                         [
516  T:                     [So you had to go back
517           in that environment and (it was a)
518                            [
519  W:                        [(It was and my) I
520           could see my son dealing with ((therapist
521           nods yes)) with what I dealt with as a kid
522           and I was like I can't do this to this
523           kid. =
524  T:      = Right ((nodding yes))
525  W:      (.hh) So, and there was other financial
526           problems ((therapist nods yes)) where I
527           couldn't get an apartment on my own or
528           anything and and (.hhh) I don't know my
529           par my mother had sat down my mother and
530           sister had sat down and said we feel that
531           you are so: depressed that you're not
532           gonna, you wouldn't be able to function on
533           your own and that you can't divide your
534           attention to your son and (.hh) so they
535           said we don't feel it's good for you to
536           get an apartment because we really fee:l
537           that =
538           [
539  T:      [right
540  W:      = possibly you're suicidal at this point, so
541           I didn't feel that I was
542                  [                    ]
543  T:             [So, (it looked like they)] were trying
544           to get the kid away: or (.1) hospital::ize
545                                 [
546  W:                            [we:ll
547  T:      you, or just say you can't be on your
548           own? =
549  W:      = Yeah, yeah,
550  T:      So: =
```

```
551  W:    = Not that I'm a nervous wreck I mean I
552             think I've handled my my son very well =
553                 [                    ]
554  T:              [right ((nodding yes)) (ok, good)]
555  W:    = and that we've done very well, =
556                 [
557  T:                 [ok, good
558  W:    ((husband nods yes)) = he's he's really
559             adjusted (.hh)
560  T:     So for financial reasons for logistic rea-
561             sons just for mechanical reasons it wa it
562             was it was better to move back together
563             (.hh) you were thinking well I'm not sure
564             I'm totally ready but it's better than all
565             the other alternatives that I can see
566             ((wife nods yes)) (.hhh) =
567  W:    = That's about where I'm at =
568                                 [
569  T:                             [ok (goo) ((nod-
570         ding yes))
571  W:    = and I know that's horrible because ((ther-
572             apist gestures as if 'who knows')) there
573             isn't (.hh) I'm not sure that there's love
574             there (.) I mean I saw so much hurt you
575             know that =
576             [
577  T:         right
578  W:    = I still (.hhh) I'm dealing with all this =
579                                     [
580  T:                                 [ok
581  W:    = and I'm just:
582  T:    Good so I: ((leans towards wife)) I think
583             that's you know I think that's important
584             to include that in there because if you're
585             (.hh) if you're just gonna say ((wife nods
586             yes)) ">Oh I'm supposed to be ((states in
587             a sing-song voice and swings his feet))
588             happy go-lucky and just supposed to go for
589             this<" then (.hhh)
590             [
591  W:         [uh hum
592  T:    obviously you're gonna start to uh you know
593             (.1) sort of (.) sort of (.) hide those parts: and say
594             "ah oh I can't really say what I feel or
595             >I can't really feel what I feel<." ((wife
596             nods yes)) (.hhh) You feel what you feel,
597             but (.h) I think we ought to be able to
```

598	inclu:de that in (.) OK we've gotta make
599	plans for: we've gotta include for those
600	goals:: (.hh) that you have if you say "OK
601	let's look at the possibility of getting
602	the two of us back together and being
603	settled ((wife nods yes)) and (.hh) moving
604	on and developing common goals and going
605	for it, (.hh) and we've gotta inclu::de
606	(.) ((points to the husband)) the hurt and
607	the upset (*>in the past<*) the doubts:
608	that you have in the present and that you
609	might have in the future (.hh) and some of
610	the >hurt that you might have in the
611	future< ((wife nods yes)) let's: inclu::de
612	that because if we leave it out it's gonna
613	come back and bonk us on the head ((wife
614	and husband nod yes)) >I think so< (.hhh)
615	Alright we'll include that. (.hhh) I think
616	you know, sometimes when I see couples
617	maybe this'll this'll make sense to you.
618	Sometimes when I see couples and things
619	have happen:ed, whatever it may be lots of
620	conflicts or affairs or whatever it may be
621	(.hhh) that (.) it's: the way I think
622	about it is sometimes when you first got
623	married when you first fell in love or
624	whatever, it's like this ((said slowly))
625	*gold:en light just sorta shinn:ed all
626	over you* ((wife nods yes)) and you felt
627	(.hhh) you know ah lov:ing and goo::d
628	((wife nods yes)) an:d clo:se to each
629	other and >all this stuff and this< (.hhh)
630	and sometimes especially when you first
631	fall in love people would look at you and
632	say ((husband nods yes)) "Boy:: what's
633	wrong with you you're glo:wing" and you
634	know, ((states in a sing-song voice)) "I'm
635	in lov::e," ((husband nods yes)) you know
636	it's really great. You you know remember
637	that feeling, where this this is just
638	glow::ing (.hh) and then:: (.4) the years
639	go on, things happen, and you know::, con-
640	flicts and all that stuff, and it's like,
641	to me, it's like ah, ah, somebody dumps a
642	pile of manure on top of the light and the
643	light sort of goes ((wife nods yes)) out
644	for awhile and you think, (.hh) "Is there

645   any light down there now? cause I can't
646   really you know like I'm saying I'm not
647   sure I lov:e him anymore" (.hhh) But the
648   way you said it is really like "is:: there
649   anything underneath that, ((wife nods
650   yes)) that manure (.) or is there not. I
651   mean do I really still love him? ((wife
652   nods yes)) >There's a lot of water under
653   the bridge I don't know whether I do or
654   not< (.hhh) ahh it's: more convenient to
655   go back at this point and it's I feel bad:
656   saying that because it sounds so you know,
657   financial or heartless, ((wife nods yes))
658   but in one way (.hh) that is the truth I
659   mean it's easier to raise your kid
660   toge:ther, it's easier financially, ((wife
661   nods yes)) it's easier in terms of living
662   situations (.hh) now you gotta figure out
663   whe:ther you still are are in here in the
664   relationship, or whether you still care
665   for for him, whether you can forgive him
666   and move on, or not, and all that stuff
667   but, (.hhh) the way I think about it is:
668   ((therapist looks down towards floor as he
669   talks)) all that cra:p, sorta that's
670   dumped on there that horse manure has to
671   be sorta washed away so you can see
672   (.hhh) is there light down ((wife nods
673   yes)) there (.1) or is there just rug down
674   there I mean is there ((wife ((wife nods
675   yes)) nothing under there. ((husband nods
676   yes)) When you, when you finally wash away
677   the problems and deal with those and move
678   on: (1.0) (.hh) then: you gotta see, is
679   there anything left in terms of of your
680   feelings? ((wife nods yes)) But for now:
681   I'd say have your doubts. And, you know, I
682   think you'd be: (.) sorta fooling yourself
683   if you said "OH, I >No, I don't have any
684   doubts< ((wife nods yes)) everything's
685   wonderful, I know exactly it's gonna work
686   out." (.hhh) ((turns to husband)) You
687   probably have your doubts too, but you're
688   I think (.hh) you've got more energy to
689   say say "I think we can make it at this
690   point, I really think we can make it".
691   (.hh) But you better ((turns to look at

```
692        wife)) include your doubts, cause, you
693        can't get rid of em just by saying ((ther-
694        apist crosses legs like wife's posture))
695        "Oh, well (.1) I I don't have any doubts
696        anymore, forget it." (1.0) Include those
697        doubts and also be able to listen to em.
698        Say, ((looks at husband)) and and don't
699        take it personally, it's like >if you
700        doubt our relationship then we don't have
701        a future< ((wife nods yes)) *No:* (.hhh)
702        (.4) you can doubt our relationship and we
703        may still have a future ((wife nods yes))
704        if we could include those doubts.
705   H:   *I used to say that. I used to wanna (1.0)
706        ((in sing-song voice)) (okey-dokey*)=
707   T:   OK, if you if you doubt then forget it,
708        we'll just s:kip it, ((husband nods yes))
709        but now you're a little more ((husband
710        nods yes)) (.1) accepting of that, and you
711        say, "OK, I realize this is what she needs
712        to have and she (what needs to do with it)
713                                     [
714   H:                               [I agree
715   T:   and if I pressure her too much, it's just
716        not it's not gonna help.
717   H:   Well, I think we (turns to look at wife))
718        talked about that every day, just about.
719        ((wife nods yes)) We'v=
720   W:   =We've made a special time every day where
721        we sit and we talk=
722                          [
723   T:                    [*Grea:t*
724   W:   =talk about our feelings and we
725                                 [
726   T:                           [OK, but does
727        that work? Is that wh is that helpful?
728                        [
729   W:                  [I think it does,
730        ((wife nods yes)) he's, I've said some
731        hurtful things, and I've I've I don't mean
732        not to hurt him but just to let him know:
733   T:   right ((nods yes))
734   W:   and I know that it's gotta hurt him (.hh)
735        but I just sit there and I say you know
736        (.hhh) I don't know if I'm as good in bed
737        with her or or as she was [or or=
738                                  [
```

739 *T:*   [And you're
740   asking him (questions) yeah, all these
741   thoughts and ( )]
742 *W:*   = and I mean I have all these things,
743   ((therapist nods yes)) and I just sit
744   there (and I)] don't wanna kno::w about
745   her but I jus I don't (.hh) I compare
746   myself I sit there and say you know >what
747   is he sitting in there thinking and you
748   know and I sit there and say "do you think
749   about her? Do you? and you know < (.hhh)
750   and he seems to be ho:nest with me you
751   know I mean we ((therapist nods yes)) we
752   talk alot but (.hh) we've realized that we
753   just can't we just moved in last week-end
754   (.hh) ((swallow)) and we just we've made
755   it a point every evening we sit down after
756   our son's in bed or whatever and we sit
757   there and we talk about either or her
758   (.hhh) or yesterday I promised ((laugh-
759   ing)) myself I ((therapist nods yes)) just
760   said today I am not gonna bring her up
761   ((therapist gestures with a slap on his
762   knee)) (laughter) and so (.hh) but um I
763   had to have =
764   [   ]
765 *T:*   [right, yeah]
766 *W:*   = one day without her (.hhh) so but um but
767   like she called two days ago and met him
768   at work
769 *T:*   right
770 *W:*   and just said I saw you guys at the mall
771   and you looked like a happy couple but,
772   ((therapist nods yes)) (.hhh) and um I'm
773   happy for you to be back together and you
774   know or something ((therapist nods yes))
775   jus::t you know, whatever, so (.hhh) =
776 *T:*   = So (um) but what I wanted to ask about
777   that day were you able to keep your vow:
778   to take one day vacation from the thoughts
779   about her: or asking about her during that
780   time? (.h)
781 *W:*   Yeah, pretty much, we ((nods yes, then
782   husband nods yes))
783   [
784 *T:*   [Was that was that good to have
785   a day off?

786 W: Yeah (.hh) ((wife nods yes)) we we talked
787   about our goals in the car on the drive
788   up up there cause our son was sleeping on
789   the way there (.hhh) and we talked about a
790   couple of goals and what we had in our
791   relationship and communication is our most
792   important thing ((therapist nods yes and
793   then husband nods yes)) (.hhh) We don't
794   tell each other how we feel we both kinda
795   locked each other up and =
796   [
797 T: [right ((nods yes))
798 W: = like he says before all this started
799   (.hhh) we we had filed ((therapist nods
800   yes)) we lost our house, we had two brand
801   new cars we were both working =
802   [
803 T: [*(oh boy)*
804 W: = he was working three jobs I was working two
805   (.hhh) and so we filed for bankruptcy so
806   we're like I mean we (laughter) ((therap-
807   ist nods yes)) started from the bottom
808   we're starting from the bottom = ((husband
809   nods yes))
810 T: = Well you know in in in another way I did
811   want to say that I've seen other people in
812   situations and sort of in in a strange way
813   I'd say (.) in a *strang:e wa:y this is
814   like an opportu:nity:* (.hh) to say OK (.)
815   now we had (.1) a marriage before (.2)
816   then: for awhile we thought ((wife nods
817   yes)) (.2) either we don't have a marriage
818   it's gonna end? or we're not sure we have
819   a marriage (.hhh) now there's an opportu-
820   nity *OK what kind of marriage do you want
821   to have?* ((wife nods yes)) (.hh) And one
822   of the things you say is (.1) we want to
823   have more communication ((wife nods yes))
824   and part of that is, >Just:! Spending
825   time together<. ((husband and wife both
826   nod yes))
827 W: Um humm
828 T: So:: it's so: making sure that you get that
829   time to spend together. ((husband nods
830   yes)) (.hhh) The other thing I think
831   you've already done, which I just wanta
832   underline, I don't know whether anybody's

833   ever told you about this is sorta ah
834   counseling technique, that's ah, that's
835   ah, I guess we it's sorta like CB radio
836   talk, it's like Wach you have to do as a
837   counselor an (.hh) you have to do more
838   than that obviously ((wife nods yes))
839   *most of the time* but one of the things
840   you have to do is make sure you hea::r
841   people. ((husband nods yes)) And let them
842   know they're heard. ((wife nods yes) An so
843   it's sorta like, "ten-four good buddy, I
844   hear the messag:e" So that may be one of
845   the challenges for you at this point
846   ((gestures to the husband)) (.hh) She's
847   got all this stuff going on ahhh you know
848   I'm thinking about her I'm scar:ed or I'm
849   upset: I have my doubts and everything
850   ((husband and wife both nod yes)) (.hhh)
851   and instead of taking it person:ally you
852   know like a counselor has to just sit back
853   and go: (.hhh) OK:, you know: that's
854   what's goin on with you, I hear what
855   you're feeling, I hear what you're saying
856   (.hhh) and it's OK: to have tha:t thought:
857   or that feeling, it's not a ba:d thing
858   (.hhh) and I don't have to take it person-
859   ally, cause sometimes in therapy people
860   wil people will (.hh) you know project all
861   sorts a things on the therapist and say
862   (.hh) (.hh) "You're just like my mother::
863   or you're just like my father ((wife nods
864   yes)) and you just have to be able
865   to say, OK I hear:: you:, you know, it's
866   OK to have those feelings, and we can be
867   here in the same room (.hh) you can be
868   angr:y at me, you can be sad:: you can be
869   you know upset: you can be distracted you
870   can be bored: whatever (.hh) and we can
871   still have this conversation. So (.hh)
872   >that's one of the challenges for you<
873   maybe for you too ((turns to wife)) is to
874   hear what's going on with him: ((wife nods
875   yes)) (.hh) and to not it personally,
876   like if he all the sudden had the thought
877   (.hh) you know, I thought about her
878   today, (.HHH) NRRR ((wife nods yes)) you
879   know push your botton you go ballistic =

880 *W:*   (laughter)
881 *T:*   = you know off you go (.hh) ((husband
882   smiles)) and say OK, in instead, sometime
883   in the future just be able to hear him say
884   (.hh) he had this random thought, ((wife
885   nods yes)) it didn't mean he's gonna go
886   bac::k with with her it didn't mean he
887   doesn't <u>lov:e</u> you, it didn't mean he's not
888   <u>committed</u> here (.hhh) but just that occa-
889   sionally he has this thought. =
890 *W:*   = Uhhuh
891 *T:*   So to be able to hear it both ways and not
892   take it personally not react ((husband
893   nods yes)) I think that (.hh), tha:t's one
894   of
895   [
896 *W:*   [(You
897   know) that was one of our I think one of
898   our big things though that led to a lot of
899   this (.hh) is: that he wasn't telling me
900   how he feel:s =
901   [
902 *T:*   [right
903 *W:*   = and like a lot of times (.hh) like last
904   week-end was very stressful we moved into
905   our apartment we all were sick with colds
906   and everything (.hhh) and he just kinda
907   phased out on me and he was just like
908   (.hhh) kinda not: ther:e and I and I says
909   (.hh) What's going on ((therapist nods
910   yes)) >how are you feeling what are you
911   doing< ((in deeper voice)) "OK (.2) I'm
912   alright OK" =
913   [
914 *T:*   [(ok)
915 *W:*   = And it's like, <u>DAMMIT!</u> I just wanna shake
916   him and say <u>Tell</u> me how you're feeling!
917   ((therapist nods yes)) I rel you know I
918   mean if it's not her fine if it's just the
919   stress of moving in ((therapist nods yes))
920   together just <u>tell</u> me what you're feeling
921   and a lot of times he doesn't do that he
922   doesn't deal with that (.hhh) =
923 *T:*   = right =
924 *H:*   = (well) I'm I'm usually the last: to know
925   how I feel
926 *T:*   ((laughter)) (yea:h right) ((slaps knee))

```
927            It's like, "huh:: I won::der ho:w ((wife
928            laughs)) I do: fee:l? ah::? goo::d ques-
929            tion::" an:d so:: ah so during those con-
930            versations though that you've had, those
931            you know sitting down every night (.hh)
932            have you been able to get a little more to
933            that?
934  H:       Sometimes.
935  T:       Sometimes, but she, ((turns to look at
936            wife)) you would be much more likely to
937            know what's goin on with you: (.hhh) an:d
938            and then you would, ((wife nods yes)) OK
939            so it takes a little practice to sorta
940            tune in to that.
941  H:       I need some kind of an exercise or some-
942            thing that would ((therapist nods yes))
943            (.6) help me (1.2) do that,
944  T:       OK
945  H:   When I can sit down and write (.5) I'm able
946            to ahh do that much better than: (.3) than
947            talking.
948  T:   Go::od, OK, so how bout keepin a journ:al?,
949            or: or actually sorta in preparation, you
950            know, sorta like ah: (.) olympic trials,
951            or something, you know in preparation
952            for:: sitting down with ah, with the two
953            of you (.hh) *you write out what's going
954            on with you whats' been going on with you
955            the last day or so: ((wife nods yes)) you
956            know ah just ten minutes ((husband nods
957            yes)) you know, just sorta* that's an
958            easier way to do it, cause sometimes:, it
959            you may notice ((wife nods yes)) (.hh)
960            that under the pressure of ((leans towards
961            husband)) > what are you feeling what are
962            you feeling what are you feeling< (.hh) I
963            mean probably what I would say is, Pres-
964            sure! ((laughs))
965  H & W:   ((wife laughs first, then husband))
966  T:   To feel something (.hh) you know that's
967            about the most I can have (open) there ahm
968            ahm, I think I ahm: you know it's it's
969            hard to to do it
970                      [
971  H:               [I feel like that sometimes.
972  T:   So:?
973  H:       Sometimes I don't feel like anything =
```

974 *T:* = Yeah, it's like ah, now I, now if I say
975   that then I'm like a dead fish, what am
976   suppos:ed to say there's no right answer
977   here, ((husband nods yes)) so, (.hh) Yeah.
978   Sorta, then going ((therapist crosses legs
979   like wife's position)) back to well: I
980   know I don't know what this second, but,
981   you know, yesterday, I was feeling kinda
982   sca:red or I: was real happy we were
983   together but I didn't wanna say that to
984   you cause I thought oh she'll just think
985   I'm you know puttin pressure on her to be
986   happy ((husband nods yes)) or whatever
987   (.hhh) >things like that<. So you know a
988   few of the things you're feeling ((husband
989   nods yes)) an:d you can articulate some of
990   those but the writing, OK, the writing may
991   help (.hhh) and that may be one of the
992   ways to do it, also something, you know,
993   it's funny that you mentioned the writing,
994   cause sometimes when I hav:e (.) (.hh)
995   couples that communicate, and sometimes
996   they get into this real blo:cked places or
997   stuck places ((wife nods yes)) in communi-
998   cating and it's like AH, we keep coming
999   back to this place and nothing seems to
1000   happen, (.hh) I just tell em OK, get a pad
1001   of paper (.) now you write out what's goin
1002   on with you or what you wanna say, and you
1003   got 5 minutes to do it you set the kitchen
1004   timer or whatever you can time it on your
1005   watch ((wife nods yes)) 5 minutes, (.hh)
1006   and then you pa pass the pad of paper to
1007   you, and then you write out wach you're
1008   what's goin on with you or ((wife nods
1009   yes)) what you wanna say in response to
1010   that or just what was goin on (.) and then
1011   you pass it back and forth. (.hh) So some-
1012   times because you're maybe a little better
1013   with ((wife nods yes)) expressing it ver-
1014   bally (.) that you know or in words, you
1015   know than in voice ((turns to look at
1016   husband)) may be a little better express-
1017   ing in writing, you may switch back and
1018   forth between those two.
1019 *W:* ((nodding yes)) We kinda, we kinda did
1020   that, just to see if we were on the same

1021		wave wave length for getting back
1022		together. We (.hhh) we ((therapist nods
1023		yes)) sat down at one point before he had
1024		moved in and we just we (.hh) we wrote
1025		down what our short term goals were and
1026		our long term goals, ((therapist nods
1027		yes)) just to see if we were on the same
1028		wave length so that we could see if we did
1029		have any thing to to to reach you know,
1030		(.hh) together, to see I don't know like
1031		financially, ((therapist nods yes)) fol-
1032		lowing a budget, be ah it's cause we both
1033		were were crazy, I mean
1034		[
1035	T:	[right ((nodding yes))
1036	W:	you wanta house fine we'll give you you 8
1037		80 thousand dollar loan
1038		[
1039	T:	[yeah
1040	W:	I mean, it just, we just got=
1041	T:	=Well you already learned the limit of
1042		that ((shakes right hand in the air))
1043	W:	((laughter)) Yeah the hard way (.hhh)
1044		[
1045	H:	[*yeah right* ((smiles))
1046	T:	H:ere, have some credit cards, yeah OK (.3)
1047		Oh wait a minute we have to pay thes:e?
1048		(laughter)
1049	W:	So (1.0) ahm (.hhh) but we we you know we
1050		did sit down and we and we worked on those
1051	T:	OK, so:: writing that stuff out was helpful,
1052		((wife nod yes)) and that's one of the
1053		parts maybe in communication that you can
1054		just can begin to build in every once in a
1055		while just sitting down and writing out
1056		what's going on with you (.hh) and where
1057		you wanna be.
1058	W:	Um hmm ((nodding yes and husband nods
1059		yes))
1060	T:	Ok. So maybe having that as a regular habit
1061		(.hh) and ahm: so (.2) ah ah how about
1062		(1.5) how::? are you gonna you know see,
1063		here's my concern, I just gonna sorta play
1064		devil's advocate (.hhh) what about (.8)
1065		things get back together, you're ((wife
1066		crosses arms over her chest)) feeling less
1067		doubts or no doubts anymore, you're feel-

```
1068              ing closer with each other things actu-
1069              ally do get back together and you're doin
1070              better (.hhh) whwhwh what will stop you
1071              from just sorta like "Well: we got busy
1072              now we don't talk anymore" ((wife nods
1073              yes)) (.3) *What will stop that?* Or what
1074              will keep it from happening do you need to
1075              ah= ((husband opens mouth as if to speak,
1076              then wife responds))
1077  W:      =To make a (.2) daily scheduled time where
1078              we have we have (        )
1079                                [        ]
1080  T:                            [(((therapist pounds fist onto
1081              his hand)) To actually make an appoint-
1082              ment] with each other and keep that
1083              appointment ((wife nods yes and unfolds
1084              her arms)) come hell or high water
1085                                          [
1086  W:                                    [We have to we
1087              just (.hhh) because:
1088                      [
1089  T:                [otherwise, it does get
1090              too busy.
1091  W:      *Yeah*
1092  H:      Before, wh when I was working two or three
1093              jobs at a time ((therapist nods yes)) and
1094              she was workin a lot=
1095  W:      =We worked opposite shifts=
1096                                  [
1097  H:                            [opposite shifts::
1098  W:      =so we wouldn't have to have child=
1099                                      [
1100  T:                                [(is that)
1101  W:      =care person we never saw each other, we
1102              probably saw one movie in the last year
1103              ((therapist nods yes)) that we were mar-
1104              ried (.hhh) we never went out to dinner
1105              ((therapist nods yes)) we never did any-
1106              thing we always just all we did was work
1107              and work and work we never (had time)=
1108  T:      =((nodding yes)) Take care of the kid and
1109              work take care of the kid work sleep (.h)
1110              ((wife and husband nod yes))
1111  W:      (and like he)
1112  H:      And gave up activities that we really
1113              enjoyed and=
1114  W:      =yeah=
```

1115 *T:*   = Well and and that's one of the other
1116   things wha:t activities have you really
1117   enjoy:ed and (.h) can you make arrange-
1118   ments to do some of them and I know child
1119   care is a concern ah maybe a little less
1120   as he grows up and he gets you know starts
1121   going to schoo:l ((husband nods yes)) and
1122   that'll take the pressure off a bit, but
1123   (.hh) ahm, what activities did you used to
1124   do or have you done recently since you've
1125   been sortof moving back together?
1126 *W:*   Together?
1127 *T:*   Yeah:: do you have any shared activities =
1128   [   ]
1129 *W:*   [It's only been a week so,
1130 *T:*   = anymore? I mean, no but I mean, as you've
1131   been sorta (.) coming back together or
1132   before what did you do either one?
1133 *W:*   We haven't really done anything he goes
1134   golfing and (.hhh)
1135 *H*   And I enjoys basketballing again =
1136 *W:*   = yeah =
1137 *H:*   = and those are the things that keep person-
1138   ally that keep me going. ((therapist nods
1139   yes))
1140 *T:*   And you that's sorta the thing that's fun =
1141   [
1142 *H:*   [But we
1143 *T:*   = for you?
1144 *H:*   Oh, yeah, but we used to enjoy, you know
1145   just going to the show.
1146 *T:*   Oh movies, yeah you said movies was one of
1147   the things =
1148 *H:*   = We've rented movies ah and sat =
1149 *W:*   (hhhhhhhh) ((wife shrugs))
1150   [
1151 *T:*   [Yeah
1152 *H:*   = and watched the movies but that's not the
1153   same thing as going =
1154 *T:*   = No, because the kids ther::e and it's you
1155   know it's it's it's difficult
1156   [
1157 *W:*   [its it's hard
1158   cause we don't have a babysitter that was
1159   one of our goals is that we would get
1160   (.hhh) find a babysitter that so we could =
1161   [   ]

```
1162  T:                         [Find some ((husband
1163          nods yes)) reliable babysitter you could
1164          count on in case]
1165  W:    = have time]
1166  T:    ok (.hhh) so you're
1167                  [
1168  H:                       [We're still on the ground
1169          floor ((therapist nods yes)) with with the
1170          planning. We had a babysitter this week-
1171          end.
1172  T:    *Oh great* =
1173  H:    = We do have to work (.) but (.2) you know
1174          tomorrow is our anniversary so we are (.4)
1175          gonna go ou:t
1176  T:    ((nodding yes)) Right you said that's:
1177                  [
1178  H:                     [So that's
1179          our plan for that and we're gonna try to
1180          do that I wanna do that once a week. (.hh)
1181  W:                       (uhm)
1182  H:    I don't work Fridays and she usually doesn't
1183          *work Fridays so*
1184                  [
1185  T:                     [OK, well you know I I can say
1186          that you know obv:iously that (.hh) ahm,
1187          dua:l caree::r you know you're both you're
1188          both workin, and things like that, and
1189          really busy, it's: tough to get, my wife
1190          and I have ah have a (.hh) sort of a (.)
1191          thing that we do I don't know if it would
1192          ever work for you, but (.hh) we we were
1193          married on the 23rd of the month (.1) an:d
1194          every 23rd of the month, ((wife nods yes))
1195          we *try and take off*, you know our sched-
1196          ules are flexible enough so that we can do
1197          that if we can't take off the 23rd we find
1198          another da::y (.hh) we call it our A day
1199          ((wife nods yes)) we write it in on =
1200  W:                       [uhm
1201  T:    = our calender first we wrote it in pencil
1202          (.3) big mistake.
1203  H & W:  (laughs)
1204  H:    right
1205  T:    Pen (.) RED pen now ((wife nods yes)) my
1206          wife went through and wrote on all:: our
1207          appointment books so we have two a piece
1208          (.hhh) =
```

1209 *W:*   =ah huh
1210 *T:*   this red ink kind of things (.8) you know, A
1211   day actually mine's in pencil in my book
1212   but I never changed that one but ah (.hhh)
1213   but the ones ((wife nods yes)) at the
1214   office so nobody can schedule appointments
1215   for us, you know, A day, A day, and we
1216   kee:p that reall:y religiously ((husband
1217   nods yes)) cause if we don't >we find that
1218   we don't<. So it's once a week, or once a
1219   month, ((wife nods yes)) and ah you know
1220   whatever: someho:w sometime (.hh) that you
1221   know, rea:lly keep it sacred (.hh) cause
1222   it's like investing, ((wife nods yes)) you
1223   know or something investing some money,
1224   ((husband nods yes)) you invest a little
1225   time in the communication into the rela-
1226   tionship (.hh) and ah (1.0) (hhh) and in
1227   the context of that relationship you'll
1228   find out whether you indeed really do want
1229   to be there I mean (.hh) maybe part of you
1230   does part of you doesn't you don't know
1231   ((wife nods yes)) for sure (.hh) now I
1232   just wanta talk a little though about (.3)
1233   leaving things behind. First of all I
1234   don't think you should trust him until
1235   you're really sure he's trustworthy, so
1236   (.) that somewhat takes time I mean when
1237   you said "Well: now I've got some evidence
1238   from her ((wife nods yes)) calling me up
1239   (.hhh) (.hhh) and now from him directly
1240   (.hh) that he's not pursuing that as far
1241   as I can tell, ((wife nods yes)) I mean
1242   you can't follow him around 24 hours a day
1243   >but as far as you can tell he's not pur-
1244   suing that< (.hhh) Now as you get more
1245   time under your belt maybe you'll feel
1246   more secur:e, that he's not pursuing that
1247   and he's reall::y trul::y ((wife nods
1248   yes)) given it up left it (.) behind. That
1249   I think is part of the healing that's part
1250   of the healing of the relationship, part
1251   of the healing of that wound whatever it
1252   may be (.hhh) that I think Time will heal
1253   some of that. (.hh) But it it may not
1254   handle all of it it may handle all of it.
1255   (.hh) If it doesn't (.5) then: what I

```
1256          think ah (.h) al:so you might consider
1257          doing is: what I've suggested to some
1258          people is (.hh) I guess just some sort of
1259          ceremon:y, I mean you when you get married
1260          you have a wedding ceremony. (.) *Right*
1261          ((wife nods yes)) (.2) (.hh) When you get:
1263          separated there's not a separation cere-
1264          mony ((wife nods yes)) (.) When there's an
1265          affair that you give up an affair:: (.)
1266          there's not a give up an affair let's get
1267          back together cermony ((wife nods yes))
1268          so:: (.hh) could you fin:d something
1269          that'd be meaningful for you: for for some
1270          people it's: renewing their marriage vows,
1271          and you know, and when you come up to
1272          that. Then you find out you know am I
1273          really READY to do this? ((wife nods yes))
1274          I mean no::? am:: I gonna say::: Yes (.) I
1275          plan to stay with you for the rest of my
1276          life or whatever you said to her you know
1277          (ahhh)
1278               [
1279   W:         [But see that's what we were talking
1280          about, we don't wear our wedding bands
1281          (.8) (.hhh) an:d he's: in a hurry to put
1282          his wedding band on: and he says =
1283                                    [
1284   T:                              [right
1285   W:    = you know I wanna I wanna be married now.
1286                              [
1287   T:                         [That may be part of
1288          the ceremony (.1) This is good. =
1289   W:    = Yea::h? But then it's like (.hhh) it's
1290          like that's fine but we put these on ONE
1291          other time:: you know, and it's
1292          like yeah, and it's        yeah =
1293          [                          ]
1294   T:    [And di:d they mea:::n anythin did it mean
1295          any anything so]
1296   W:    = proven to me 6 years that nothing you know =
1297                    [
1298   T:               [good
1299   W:    = and I find a real hard time dealing with
1300          tha:t. (.hhh) =
1301   T:    = good, so don't put em on before you're
1302          ready ((wife nods yes)) (1.0) Now: (1.0)
1303          HOW:: will you know you're ready? Will it
```

1304		be fee::ling will it be some more tim::e
1305		(.hh) will it be something else that needs
1306		to happen so that that I that I actually
1307		think (.hh) if you could possibly arrange
1308		it would be part of the ceremony, is the
1309		exchanging of rings again ((Husband and
1310		wife both nod yes)) (1.0) But really
1311		having the other person put it on with
1312		your permission not like (.hh) here ((wife
1313		nods yes)) (.hh) I'm gonna jam this on
1314		your finger cause I think it needs that =
1315		((gestures jamming it into his finger))
1316	W:	= Well we wrote our own
1317		[
1318	T:	[You'd love to have it
1319		happen yesterday, right? ((turns to look
1320		at husband))
1321	W:	((laughs))
1322	T:	You wrote your own (.) ceremony?
1323	W:	Wedding vows, that kind of thing,
1324		[
1325	T:	[OK, maybe you
1326		need to either rewrite them, or you need
1327		to look at those and see (.hh) Now:: you
1328		know, OK that one was a practice run
1329		((husband and wife nod yes)) am I
1330		really committed to these now?
1331	W:	(laughs)) that's what I mean that (.h) how
1332		do I know that he's serious about th =
1333	T:	= Well: that's a goo:d ((nodding yes))
1334		questio:n? how would you know? I mean you
1335		only know over time ultimately you can't
1336		really tell beforehand (.) BUT (.hhh) you
1337		know do you think he's really serious this
1338		time? (1.0) You know, he ple:d termporary
1339		insanity and maybe immaturity I didn't
1340		(.hh) you know, I real:ly didn't know:?
1341		(there is)
1342		[
1343	W:	[She had a lot of things,
1344		like we've talked about what drove him to
1345		her, and everything and (.hhh) and like
1346		she lived ((therapist nods yes)) on wel-
1347		fare she's a unwed mother she has a child
1348		of her of her own and everything (.hhh)
1349		but it was just it (.hh) she didn't

```
1350            require anything of him. And in our
1351            stressful lives =
1352                [
1353  T:            [sure
1354  W:     = we were filing for bankruptcy ((therapist
1355            nods yes)) we were doing we were reaching
1356            so many goals and like here she is sitting
1357            here ready for him at any time of day you
1358            know (.hhh) =
1359  T:     = right =
1360  W:     = she's always there when he calls she's
1361            alway::s there and
1362                        [
1363  T:                    [Not that many demands =
1364  W:     = yep it was there was nothin he could come
1365            and go ((therapist nods yes)) if he
1366            decided they weren't gonna go out to din-
1367            ner that night they were going to go he
1368            was gonna go golfing with his friends
1369            (.hh) he got to do that ((therapist nods
1370            yes)) and in my in my relationship (.hh) I
1371            mean I required him I said no dammit
1372            ((therapist nods yes)) you're not going
1373            out golfing tonight cause you have to =
1374                [
1375  T:            [right
1376  W:     = babysit cause I have to work or whatever. =
1377  T:     = You know tal::k with me: or whatever yeah,
1378            there was more pressure
1379                    [
1380  W:                [So:: it was like it was
1381            you know I can I can see his point with
1382            that but I just still I get angry because
1383            he pleads temporary insanity with the the
1384            hurt that he had done to me.
1385  T:     Sure right.
1386  W:     So =
1387  H:     = But I feel it all now too: you know, I
1388            didn't feel anything when I was doin that
1389            (.hhh) but now I every day I still =
1390                        [
1391  T:                    [Yeah
1392  H:     = feel that.
1393  T:     Yeah, so you say I'm goin through some pain
1394            too OK so:: (.hh) alright (1.0) so (.4)
1395            the question is (.) what would it take to
```

```
1396              be ready to (.2) *put that ring on again?*
1397              (2.0) Will it tak:e (1.2) more communica-
1398              tion? (.1) will it take more time? (.8)
1399              How:: can (.) he sho:w you (.2) tha:t (.)
1400              he's really committed this >time? is<
1401              there a way that you can think of that he
1402              can show you or again will it be time?
1403              (.hhh)
1404   W:         (.hhh) I think it's gonna be time cause
1405              even (.hhh) ((therapist nods yes)) =
1406   T:     (good)
1407   W:    = his his job is on (.hhh) his job is on call
1408              and he gets phone calls and it's it's
1409              girls ((therapist nods half yes and no))
1410              that call because they he works he's a
1411              orderly and he works you know (.hhh) and =
1412                         [
1413   T:                   [right
1414   W:    = the girls call and say we need you =
1415                      [
1416   T:               [so:
1417   W:    = someone's gotta go to the hospital and he
1418              has to go there.
1419   T:     So eventually if he if he really: you know
1420              if he's really fool:ing you * you'll find
1421              out.*
1422   W:        It well (.hh) (if he)
1423                    [
1424   T:             [It it'll emerge.
1425   W:        Another thing that he that just kinda scared
1426              me and I was like GOD what is what is he
1427              doing ((therapist nods yes)) you know
1428              (.hhh) cause he said if you don't trust me
1429              feel free to call anytime and he goes I
1430              want you to check up on me ((therapist
1431              nods yes)) if it makes you feel better =
1432   T:    = sure ((nodding yes)) =
1433   W:    = (.hh) I'm like does he want me to check up
1434              on him because he (.) doesn't (.) trust
1435              himself or does he want me to check up on
1436              him to make me feel better? ((therapist
1437              nods yes)) (.hhh) You know =
1438   T:    = Let's ask him. ((gestures to the husband))
1439   W:        (hhh) I know my answer already.
1440   T:     Yeah:: what's the answer?
1441                               [
1442   H:                         [I want I want you to
```

```
1443          check up on me so you'll feel better? =
1444          ((wife nods yes))
1445  T:    = It's funny that you say that because that's
1446          sometimes what I assign to people I see
1447          you know the wa̱y: to establish trust (.hh)
1448          h:ow you know a person's trustworthy is
1449          consistent behavior of the kin::d that you
1450          want
1451                                      [
1452  W:                        [But I'm
1453          paranoid I'm (   )
1454                        [
1455  T:                [Over time (ahh) I mean you
1456          can feel that but (.2) what what the heck
1457          you know your your mind just well it takes
1458        [
1459  W:    [Well, if he got called he had to get
1460          someone to the hospital     and so
1461                            [
1462  T:                    [((nodding yes)) right
1463          and so he's saying lookit I (.2) I:: trust
1464          that if you call up (.) I'll always be
1465          where I say I'll be and I won't be where I
1466          say I won't be.
1467  W:          uh umm ((nodding yes))
1468  T:    >You know< so check on me because I:'m
1469          committed to you finding out that I'm
1470          trustworthy ((wife nods yes)) (.hhh) and
1471          you're saying OK over time (.hhh) maybe I
1472          can really trust that (.)     Right now I
1473          trust it a liddle (.3) b:::ut? (.3) maybe
1474          what would happen if he has another tempo-
1475          rary bout of insanity ((wife nods yes)) he
1476          no he would just go "OH >I'm insane
1477          again<" (     )
1478  W:    ((laughs)) see you later (I know)
1479  T:    Yeah; so you don't know but I think that:
1480          (.) obviously as tim::e goes on you know
1481          if you got into an elevator (.4) (.hhh)
1482          and you got on the elevator and you've
1483          ridden 100 elevators and you everything
1484          went fine you got in the elevator one time
1485          and the cable snapped and you fell down
1486          ((wife nods yes)) (.hhh) and you survived
1487          (.8) mean: (.) if you actually had to ride
1488          an elevator again or decided you know I
1489          need to overcome this this fear (.) how:
```

1490		many times would it take for you to ride
1491		the elevator ((wife nods yes)) before you
1492		trusted it again? (.hhh) Probably not the
1493		first time ((wife nods yes)) (.2) Probably
1494		not the first week (.2) Probably not the
1495		first month (1.0) Then after that after
1496		if you've ridden it a number of times
1497		maybe you'd start to say well: (.) (.h) ok
1498		maybe I can stop sort of holding on to the
1499		walls: her:e and clawing on to things
1500		(.hhh) maybe you'd start to trust (.) you
1501		know and (.) but ultimately the elevator
1502		can fall *at any time* (.) *right* It
1503		could (.4) It's always a risk you take
1504		(.2) (.hh) But in any relationship you're
1505		gonna take that risk if you have a rela-
1506		tionship with somebody (.hhh) you could
1507		be betrayed: you could be hu::rt they
1508		could have an affair:: they could leav::e
1509		they could di::e (.2) anything. It's
1510		possible (.3) Now: are: you willing to
1511		live with that risk an:d how: long will it
1512		take before you really are ready to say
1513		"OK (.) (.hh) I'm not sure I was: really
1514		ready to be back in or not now I'm ready
1515		to be back in here" So: you (.hh) don't
1516		put on that ring before that ((wife nods
1517		yes)) (1.0) ((therapist turns to husband))
1518		You know you and you'd love her to put it
1519		on yesterday *right?* =
1520	*H:*	= *right* ((nodding yes))
1521	*T:*	But (.2) if you p:ut it on before she's
1522		ready (.2) *it ain't gonna do ((husband
1523		shakes head no)) it* you know she's gonna
1524		feel the pressure then (.hh) the doubts
1525		and fears ((husband nods yes)) I think'll
1526		be more >so don't put it on< (.hhh) Is
1527		there anything else you can do like (.1)
1528		and I'm just gonna give you a few sugges-
1529		tions (.hhh) I think of one particular
1530		case in which ah (.2) a couple that I knew
1531		(.h) she had an affair with a guy (.2)
1532		and she had a collection of (.2) unicorns.
1533		This was her thing she collected unicorns.
1534		And the guy she had an affair with GAVE
1535		her some unicorns course that were pretty
1536		special to her ((wife nods yes)) because

1537		this guy <u>gave</u> it to her (.hhh) Now this
1538		guy (.) she was married to: Found out
1539		about it. Now they got back together
1540		eventually (.hh) she gave up the affair
1541		(1.0) bu:t he said *you know: ((wife nods
1542		yes)) (.1) I can't <u>handle</u> you having those
1543		unicorns* (.hh) and she said well <u>that's</u>
1544		<u>my unicorn collection</u> you know I've col-
1545		lected em for <u>years</u> (.hhh) he said (.hhh)
1546		those particular unicorns I ((husband nods
1547		yes)) <u>just can't handle you having</u> em she
1548		said I don't think you should ask me to
1549		give that up (.hhh) and he said (.2) *I'm
1550		afraid I'm gonna have to insist* ((wife
1551		nods yes)) and she said you can't control:
1552		me (.hh) and we did negotiate it he says
1553		<u>that</u> seems to me to be <u>such</u> a symbol of
1554		the affair (.1) that *<u>that</u>* those unicorns
1555		and (.hhh) so ultimately (.hhh) she really
1556		had to think about it they were tough for
1557		her to give up (.) but she gave them up
1558		(.3) And they went out and buried them
1559		together ((wife nods yes)) (.4) Which for
1560		them was like (.2) you know <u>burying this</u>
1561		this (.hhh) is there <u>anything</u> that you
1562		((wife stretches then crosses arms over
1563		chest)) can think of or that you can think
1564		of that might serve as a almost a concrete
1565		symbol for that (.hh) that you could go
1566		<u>burn:</u> or <u>bury</u> or (.hhh) <u>throw off</u> the pier
1567		((wife uncrosses arms)) or: throw in the
1568		the lake or whatever it may be anything
1569		(.hhh) and <u>I</u> would prefer it (.) just
1570		because I'm sort of perverse in this
1571		(.hhh) something that would be very diffi-
1572		cult for you to give up I just just
1573		because I think that sort of poetically
1574		fits =
1575	W:	=I don't think he has anything physical
1576		from her (.hhh) ((husband shakes head no))
1577		and as soon as we get
1578		[
1579	T:	[No letters no:: ((wife
1580		shakes head no)) ah <u>pho:tos::</u>
1581	W:	This this is what I did is when we got back
1582		together I ((laughs)) [searched his room
1583		left and right] ((therapist shakes his

```
1584                  hands back and forth, laughs and then hus-
1585                  band laughs))
1586              [                          ]
1587    T:       [(                      )] ((laughs)) I'm
1588                  getting this stuff and (she)=
1589    W:          =And she smoked, ((therapist nods yes))
1590                  and like alll of our cars are are you know
1591                  his car is like full of =
1592                      [                       ]
1593    T:              [smell like smoke yes] ((husband
1594                  looks back and forth between wife and
1595                  therapist))
1596    W:       =cigarettes and stuff so >I wiped (.hhh)
1597                  clean the astray and threw those out and
1598                  everything< and (   )
1599                              [
1600    T:                       [Oh I wish you'd kept
1601                  those maybe put em on
1602                          [
1602    W:                    [No (                    )
1604                              [                    ]
1605    T:                       [no no no that's OK
1606    W:       But there's ah I've searched high and low
1607                  there's =
1608              [
1609    T:       [right
1610    W:          =no letters that I know of there's ahm=
1611                  ((husband shakes his head no))
1612    T:       =Yaahm:: (.5) OK (.hhh) so maybe there's
1613                  nothing physical like that ((wife nods
1614                  yes)) (.hhh)
1615                      [
1616    W:              [(I don't think so)]
1617    T:       ahm (.4) I ah another thing that I've sug-
1618                  gested with people maybe you'll come
1619                  across something like that or she'll write
1620                  a letter or something and then you'll have
1621                  one of those thing ((wife nods yes)) so:
1622                  sav:e it and burn it or bury it
1623                              [
1624    W:                       [Well, I do hav:e a $48
1625                  dozen ros:e bill that's written to her
1626                  with her name on it we can burn that we
1627                  can (.hhh)=
1628    T:       =Good ((husband nods yes)) I like that
1629                  alright OK so
1630                      [
```

```
1631  W:                    [I had a baby to get a dozen
1632                 roses I don't know what she did to get a
1633                 dozen roses, =
1634            [                                    ]
1635  T:       [((laughs)) ((laughs and claps hands))
1636  W:       I don't think that's fair at all.   ((laughs
1637                 and then husband laughs))
1638  T:     OK, ((therapist and wife both laughing))
1639                 right ah: oh good so that ooh that's a
1640                 good one I like that you actuall:y got the
1641                 bill of sale I like that.
1642                    [
1643  W:                 [I can be devious when I want =
1644  T:      that's good =
1645  W:      = I got all the mail when we moved out of our
1646                 house so that is in =
1647                    [
1648  T:                 [Right      = so hey, you =
1649  W:      = (   ) I remember that day I called up and
1650                 said =
1651  T:      = Maybe you should hire yourself out as a
1652                 private detective ((wife laughs)) you're
1653                 pretty good I like that you got (.hh) ah
1654                 (.hh) you got that ability to gather all
1655                 the information.
1656                    [            ]
1657  W:                 [I just didn't want him to just just be::
1658                 ((therapist nods yes)) (.hhh) you know
1659                 somewhere in his room and then run up on
1660                 something and say hey I'll give her a call
1661                 cause and see what she's =
1662                    [
1663  T:                 [right    ((nodding yes))
1664  W:      = doin you know =
1665  T:      = Exactly =
1666  W:      = I just wanted to get everything out of
1667                 there I wanted to just wash =
1668                    [           ]
1669  T:                 [Clean it out
1670  W:      = her away =
1671  T:      = Ok but it that's an interesting you wanted
1672                 to wash her away because that was the next
1673                 thing I was gonna suggest (.hhh) I've had
1674                 som:e people (.) that I suggested ok *do a
1675                 ceremony* and the ceremony is: get a bunch
1676                 of candles and put them around the bathtub
1677                 (1.0) and then:: decide which one of you
```

1678	goes in first (.) or which one of you goes
1679	in (.hh) have a bath that's a ritual
1680	cleaning (.) ((wife nods yes)) its like
1681	(.hh) le lets you want to wash her out of
1682	your life ((wife nods yes)) I mean that is
1683	exactly what I'm talking about (.hhh) <u>wash</u>
1684	this off (.4) now <u>man</u>:: do it f f for
1685	goo::d or it may not do it forever or it
1686	<u>may</u> it <u>may</u> some<u>thing</u> that you can ((wife
1687	nods yes)) <u>do</u>:: I mean they're saying
1688	(.hhh) >I'm sitting here with all these
1689	feelings what can I do?< ((wife nods yes))
1690	(.hh) that may be one thing an and again:
1691	you'll find ou:t as you approach that. Am
1692	I really <u>will:ing</u> *to do this* is this
1693	something I'm willing to do am I willing
1694	to let go of some of that (.hh) or am I
1695	willing to forgiv:e or am I willing to
1696	<u>leave</u> it in the past ((wife nods yes))
1697	(.2) am I willing to yet: (.3) so (1.0)
1698	decide who goes in firs:t (.) make it a
1699	real (.) solemn ceremony who goes in first
1700	or which one of you has to go in ((wife
1701	nods yes)) (.hh) an it may be washing the
1702	affair off of you it may be washing the
1703	(.hhh) anger or the you know the (.hh)
1704	hate off you or whatever it may be or
1705	(.hhh) you know bathing in forgiveness or
1706	whatever it may be then you get out (.hh)
1707	and then the other person dries you off
1708	((wife nods yes)) (1.0) Some<u>thing</u> like
1709	that (.1) ((wife nods yes)) maybe <u>that</u> it
1710	may be something like that (.hhh) some-
1711	thing you can do:: concretely to symbolize
1712	OK you know in (.hh) in other cultures
1713	they have these rites: of passage ((hus-
1714	band nods yes)) you know and you have to
1715	go through this: or become ah (.hhh) from
1716	an adolescent to an adu:lt or you know a
1717	marriag:e ceremoni:es ((wife nods yes)) or
1718	whatever it may be or:: (.hhh) things like
1719	that we don't have much of that especially
1720	around this kind of stuff: ((husband nods
1721	yes)) (.hhh) <u>How</u> can you find a way:: to
1722	really declare (.4) this (.) I I'm ready
1723	to let this one go or <u>wash</u> ((wife nods
1724	yes)) this one away or <u>I</u> <u>intend</u> to wash

1725	this away (1.0) ((therapist looks at hus-
1726	band and then the husband nods yes)) so
1727	moving back together is: sort of a ritual
1728	(.) and going through the step ((wife nods
1729	yes)) and (.hhh) gedding rid of whatever
1730	is another ritual (.hhh) gedding rid of
1731	the cigarettes out of the car is another
1732	ritual that's a way ((wife nods yes)) to
1733	sort of declare (.hhh) ok that was our
1734	life then: (.hh) and we can (.) and now
1735	we: want to set our sights on the future
1736	and on our goals: that you have written
1737	down together ((wife nods yes)) and talked
1738	about yesterday: in the car (.hhh) and all
1739	that (.1) an::d we want to move towards
1740	that that doesn't mean we can't have some
1741	of the fee:lings from the old times: that
1742	doesn't mean we can't have some of the
1743	doubts: and fears:: and (.hhh) and all
1744	that: (.1) but (.3) we're to going to
1745	declare that we're in this together and
1746	we're going for ((wife nods yes)) it (.hh)
1747	(1.3) and at any moment (.2) you could
1748	bail out or you could bail out that always
1749	a possibility but at least you declare
1750	here's our intention to go (1.0) towards
1751	getting back together (1.1) ok (.2) so
1752	(.hhh) given what we talked about I mean
1753	we are obviously not going to handle
1754	every:thing in the world: in (.hh) in this
1755	particular consultation but I want to find
1756	out is there anything else (.hh) that you
1757	need to sa::y or that I need to hear about
1758	or that we need t to talk about (.hh) and
1759	ahh you know th the people who invited you
1760	here will be hearing this:: and (.hh) some
1761	of them may be able to follow up ((wife
1762	nods yes)) on you know and give you some
1763	consultation (.hhh) if you'd like to come
1764	back again: and or check in with you about
1765	this stuff or other things but given wh
1766	what the time we have here (.hhh) and what
1767	we were doing here anything else that you
1768	want to say or need to say or ask or do or
1769	whatever *while we're here*
1770	(2.0)
1771 W:	((Husband looks towards wife as if for her

```
1772              to answer)) *I I don't know* (2.1) *I
1773              think I gotten pretty much what I want out
1774              ((therapist nods yes and husband nods
1775              yes)) and I don't know*
1776   T:      *Ok* (.hhh) =
1777   W:    = Then I asked him and that's what bothers me
1778              most ((folds arms over chest)) is just the
1779              trust in him (.hhh) =
1780   T:        = yeah right ((nodding yes, coughs)) =
1781   W:      = how to build that back thats what I have
1782              to do before I can do anything I I feel
1783              that's important like before I can go any-
1784              where ((unfolds her arms from chest))
1785              (.hhh) is to get that trust back
1786   T:      right and and you know as much as you
1787              doubted maybe his motives I think that
1788              what he offered is (.hh) is what is an
1789              essential key (.2) to be able to check up
1790              on him any time you may ((wife nods yes))
1791              think "AWWW I shouldn't be so paranoid I
1792              shouldn't have to check up ((wife nods
1793              yes)) (on him) does he think he is not
1794              trustworthy" (.hhh) I think his statement
1795              was "I'm trustworthy now I want you to
1796              kno::w I'm trustworthy ((wife nods yes))
1797              to really find it out and if you need to
1798              check up on me that's what you need to do =
1799   W:      = that's what we do that's (        )
1800                                        [
1801   T:                                   [cause (.) I
1802              can't find a way to prove it to you other
1803              than that =
1804   H:        = (that's what)
1805                            [
1806   T:                      [but you know I can tell::: you
1807              a hundred times I'm trustworthy I'm trust-
1808              worthy ((wife nods yes)) you can trust me
1809              now (.hh) I'm really in here but (.) (.hh)
1810              either his actions don't support it (.hh)
1811              it doesn't mean a thing and he's ((wife
1812              nods yes)) saying (.hhh) "I'm::: saying my
1813              actions support it you can check up on me
1814              ANY moment (.) ((wife nods yes)) abso-
1815              lutely.
1816   W:      There is a kinda negative side to things
1817              like (.1) this you know I always: (.hh)
1818              pull from the negative I know I never look
```

1819		at anything positive you know I say well
1820		he's not saying this for me to check up on
1821		him he's saying this because he he doesn't
1822		trust himself I always look at things that
1823		[
1824	*T:*	[I
1825		actually heard you say both I heard you
1826		say ((wife chuckles)) "Now is he doing it
1827		be:caus::e he rea::ly doesn't think He's
1828		trustworthy or ((wife nods yes)) is he
1829		doing it to help me establish the trust"
1830		so I I think maybe you look at both sides
1831		of it ((wife nods yes)) now maybe you
1832		DWELL: a liddle more on the negative =
1833		[
1834	*W:*	[(yeah I do
1835		((nodding yes))
1836	*T:*	= especially when you're upset =
1837	*W:*	= yeah.
1838	*T:*	You dwell maybe on the on the on: the nega-
1839		tive side of it (.hhh) but you know I
1840		think that that's the challenge of: your
1841		relationship he's gotta be able to include
1842		that: (.3) or:: he's not going to have a
1843		relationship ((wife nods yes)) with you
1844		you better be able to include the negative
1845		side to that which is one of things you've
1846		been dealing with (.hhhh) and you better
1847		be able to include the the down sides of
1848		the pressures of being married and (.hhh)
1849		having financial difficulties or having a
1850		kid or whatever it may be (.hhh) or it's
1851		not for you (.1) you know marriage isn't
1852		for you (.) obviously (.hh) having an
1853		affair is almost always easier it's like
1854		the person is really grea:t: or sexually
1855		exciting: their ne::w you know and (.hhh)
1856		no demands or very few demands ((wife nods
1857		yes)) (.hhh) actually as time goes on
1858		sometimes there are more demands and you
1859		start to say (.hh) this looking more and
1860		more like this: and so you start to say
1861		(.hh) all of the benefits that I got from
1862		the marriage (1.1) the the it's not being
1863		outweighed anymore by the benefits from
1864		this: and one of the things that I want is
1865		a relationship that you know (.hhh) with

1866	somebody that I had a <u>child</u> with I want a
1867	relationship with somebody that I (.hh)
1868	think will be <u>stable</u> and will last for a
1869	long time somebody who has the ((wife nods
1870	yes)) kind of qualities that you have and
1871	that we can have the kinda life that we
1872	were building together (.hhh) and you made
1873	the decision I wanna go back in this
1874	direction (.hhh) you've <u>tentatively</u> sort
1875	of said <u>I'll think</u> ((wife nods yes))
1876	about <u>making</u> this decision and (.hhh)
1877	your: actions seem to support that now
1878	you'll see see whether ultimately this is
1879	the *kinda marriage you want to have?*
1880	(.1) (.hh) or you want to to be married.
1881	((husband nods yes))
1882 W:	(.hh) Well I think I I was always happy
1883	with him and I loved him ((therapist nods
1884	yes)) and I always (.hhh) but he we always
1885	I mean we were always the the easy going
1886	couple we always worked ((therapist nods
1887	yes)) in the same places so everybody knew
1888	us and everybody was like <u>Oh My God Donald</u>
1889	<u>did that</u> >I mean because ( ) even if
1890	somebody told me this was going to happen
1891	five years ago I was like (.hhh) Donald
1892	would never hurt me Donald would ((therap-
1893	ist nods yes)) <u>never</u> do that to me no you
1894	know (.hhh) it was like I just really
1895	(.hhh) and even now< ( )
1896	[[ ]
1897 T:	[And he probably would
1898	have said that too
1899 H:	Yeah ((nodding yes))=
1900 W:	=Yeah (.3) I guess
1901 H:	( )
1902 T:	It's an optio he's not the kinda guy I ( )=
1903 W:	=But now that I see that it is happening I
1904	seen him come from the normal person that
1905	I know into what he he was the last eight
1906	months (.hhh) and I'm like (.hhh) you
1907	know <u>God</u> that's so <u>unstable</u> and I don't
1908	know if <u>I</u> can live with that instability
1909	you know I don't know if I can I can live
1910	with knowing that he can (.hhh) just walk
1911	out and do this and it's not only me that
1912	he hurt I mean our son had some challenges

1913	too ((therapist nods yes)) I mean people
1914	say oh he's too (young) he doesn't know
1915	(.hhh) but he <u>knew</u>: and it it was it was
1916	tough on him for awhile too ((therapist
1917	nods yes)) so (.hhh) and I say how can=
1918	[
1919	T: [Sure
1920	W: =my husband who is supposed to love his <u>son</u>
1921	do this to him <u>too</u> ((therapist nods yes))
1922	you know (.hh) because (just)
1923	[
1924	T: [so have those
1925	thoughts have thos:::e criticisms have
1926	those fears and include those (.hhh) and
1927	that's one of things to include in your
1928	nightly conversation ((wife nods yes))
1929	(.hh) even if you think ((in sing-song
1930	voice)) "Oh I should be done with this
1931	no:w I shouldn't be thinking ((wife nods
1932	yes)) about this I shouldn't be saying
1933	this DADADDAD" >even if you think< oh I
1934	wish she'd get through this (.hhh)
1935	W: ((laughter)) While I was talking
1936	[
1937	T: [I wish you
1938	could do
1939	W: ((laughing)) I go do you do you do I drive
1940	you crazy bringing her up everyday and he
1941	says (.hhh) he says well to tell you the
1942	truth I don't think about her until you
1943	<u>bring her up</u> ((laughing)) ( )
1944	[
1945	T: [((therapist laughs,
1946	then husband looks at therapist and hus-
1947	band smiles)) Yeah right you sorta
1948	reminded me of her <u>don't do that!</u> you know
1949	I was trying to get over it myself: and
1950	everyday: (.hhh) Well so I also would sug-
1951	gest you know if that's the case and if
1952	that's the case for you (.hhh) just chose
1953	one night one day a week and take a vaca-
1954	tion from it (.2) take a vacation thinking
1955	((wife nods yes)) about it if you <u>can</u>
1956	(.hhh) but certainly take a vacation from
1957	disscussing it say *OK (.2) <u>this</u> day she
1958	we declare she is not going to be in our
1959	lives* ((wife nods yes)) (1.1) be because

1960		you don't wanna throw it all out together
1961		because then maybe he'll just be <u>denying</u>
1962		((wife nods yes)) whacha feeling whacha
1963		thinking (.hhh) and that probably won't
1964		work >ultimately< ((husband nods yes)) but
1965		in in the interim you can take a vacation
1966		then you might stretch it to a two day
1967		((wife nods yes)) vacation then a three
1968		day vacation (.hh) till you're ready to
1969		let go of it all together. ((husband nods
1970		yes))
1971		[
1972	W:	[uh huh
1973	T:	(.) Until it's <u>finally</u> ((wife nods yes))
1974		in the past, it's history (1.1) so (1.0)
1975		(.hh) you thought you knew what the norm
1976		was in your marriage (.2) and the norm
1977		changed and we'll see if we can find a new
1978		norm: for your marriage (.) right.
1979	W:	(.hhh) I want the old one back.
1980	T:	((laughing)) (.hh) You want the old one
1981		back =
1982	W:	=I want the old and reliable
1983		[ ]
1984	H:	=[I want a new and improved one.]
1985	T:	You want a new and improved one. >He <u>she</u><
1986		does?
1987	H:	I do!
1988	T:	You do?
1989	H:	I want myself to be =
1990	T:	=Yeah Ok so the best of the old one ((hus-
1991		band nods yes)) (.hh) BUT (.2) see I don't
1992		want the old one back exactly (.2) cause I
1993		want the ol::d one (.1) with:: a clear::
1994		commitment that he is here ((wife nods
1995		yes)) (1.2) So we'll take the old one (.2)
1996		new and r:r:re:r:revis::ed or whatever the
1997		>revised edition< ((husband and wife both
1998		nod yes)) I want the second edition.
1999	H:	Right!
2000	T:	>Yeah ok< (.hhhh) so: we'll see if we can
2001		establish a new norm in this relationship
2002		*right?*
2003	H:	*right* ((nodding yes))
2004	T:	*alright good* (1.0) (.hhhh) <u>Alright</u> well
2005		now the invitation ahh we: just talked
2006		briefly before we started was: that your

2007		welcome to:: (.2) umm go home do what you
2008		need to do you're welcome to come down:
2009		(.hh) in the room sit in back of the room
2010		(.hh) and listen to ahh a few minutes of
2011		discussion I I don't know how long we will
2012		discuss it we may move on to other things
2013		(.hhhh) you're welcome to sit in the <u>front</u>
2014		of the room and answer questions:: cause
2015		some people may have questions for you::
2016		What are you most comfortable with? So::
2017	W:	I would like to go and answer (.) a couple
2018		of questions just for a liddle while and
2019		(that will be a good experience to do)
2020		((looks at husband))
2021		[
2022	H:	[*ok sure* (husband nods yes))
2023		[ ]
2024	T:	[ok good that will help their
2025		learning ( ) now I want to say <u>what</u> did
2026		you: feel: or how did you perceive this
2027		((wife nods yes)) probably they're prob-
2028		ably they're going to have some ( )
2029	W:	Ok
2030	T:	Maybe they won't and maybe ahh
2031	W:	How do you feel? ((turns to husband))
2032	H:	That's fine with me.
2033	T:	((laughing)) Fine with you, OK.
2034		[ ]
2035	W:	[((laughing)) (that's what I want)
2036	T:	Ok lets go
2037	W:	( )
2038	T:	Yeah right, we were just assuming you were
2039		going to go along with us.
2040	((they all stand and move off camera))	

References

Anderson, C. M. (1988). The selection of measures in family therapy research. In L. C. Wynne (Ed.), *The state of the art in family therapy research: Controversies and recommendations* (pp. 81–88). New York: Family Process Press.

Andreozzi, L. L. (1985). Why outcome research fails the family therapist. In L. L. Andreozzi (Ed.), *Integrating research and clinical practice* (pp. 1–9). Rockville, MD: Aspen Publication.

Auerswald, R. G. (1988). Epistemological confusion and outcome research. In L. C. Wynne (Ed.), *The state of the art in family therapy research: Controversies and recommendations* (pp. 55–74). New York: Family Process Press.

Austin, J. L. (1975). *How to do things with words: Second edition*. Cambridge, MA.: Harvard University Press. (Original work published in 1962)

Barlow, D. H. (1981). On the relation of clinical research to clinical practice: Current issues, new directions. *Journal of Counseling and Clinical Psychology, 49*, 142–155.

Bateson, G. (1972). *Steps to an ecology of mind*. New York: Ballantine Books.

Bateson, G. (1977). The growth of paradigms for psychiatry. In P. Ostwald (Ed.), *Communication and social interaction: Clinical and therapeutic aspects of human behavior* (pp. 331–337). New York: Grune & Stratton.

Bateson, G. (1979). *Mind and nature: A necessary unity*. Toronto: Bantam Books.

Bergin, A. E., & Strupp, H. H. (1972). *Changing frontiers in the science of psychotherapy*. Chicago: Aldine Atherton.

Birdwhistle, R. L. (1970). *Kinesics and context: Essays on body motion communication*. Philadelphia: University of Pennsylvania Press.

Buttny, R. (1990). Blame-accounts sequences in therapy: The negotiation of relational meanings. *Semiotica, 78*, 219–247.

Buttny, R., & Lannamann, J. W. (1987). *Framing problems: The hierarchical organization of discourse in a family therapy session*. Unpublished manuscript.

Davis, K. (1984). The process of problem (re)formulation in psychotherapy. *Sociology of Health and Illness, 8*, 44–74.

de Shazer, S. (1982). Some conceptual distinctions are more useful than others. *Family Process, 21*(71), 71–84.

de Shazer, S. (1985). *Keys to solution in brief therapy*. New York: W. W. Norton & Company.

Duncan, S., Rice, L. N., & Butler, J. M. (1968). Therapist's paralanguage in peak and poor psychotherapy hours. *Journal of Abnormal Psychology, 73*, 566–570.

Elliott, R. (1983). Fitting process research to the practicing psychotherapist. *Psychotherapy: Theory, Research and Practice, 20*(1), 47–55.

Elliott, R. (1984). A discovery-oriented approach to significant change events in psychotherapy: Interpersonal process recall and comprehensive process analysis. In L. N. Rice & L. S. Greenberg (Eds.), *Patterns of change: Intensive analysis of psychology process* (pp. 249–286). New York: The Guilford Press.

Elliott, R. (1986). Interpersonal process recall (IPR) as a psychotherapy process research method. In L. S. Greenberg & W. M. Pinsof (Eds.), *The psychotherapeutic process: A research handbook* (pp. 503–528). New York: The Guilford Press.

Erickson, M. H. (1980). *The collected papers of Milton H. Erickson on hypnosis, Volumes I to IV* (Ernest L. Rossi, Ed.). New York: Irvington.

Gale, J. E., & Brown-Standridge, M. D. (1988). Ratification and utilization: Hypnotic techniques to facilitate reframing during early marital therapy. *Journal of Marital and Family Therapy, 14*(4), 371–382.

Garfinkel, H. (1967). *Studies in ethnomethodology.* Englewood Cliffs, NJ: Prentice-Hall.

Gilbert, G. N., & Mulkay, M. (1984). *Opening Pandora's box: A sociological analysis of scientists' discourse.* Cambridge: Cambridge University Press.

Gill, M., Newman, R., & Redlich, F. C. (1954). *The initial interview in psychiatric practice.* New York: International Universities Press, Inc.

Glaser, B. G., & Strauss, A. L. (1967). *The discovery of grounded theory: Strategies for qualitative research.* Chicago: Aldine Publishing Company.

Goffman, E. (1981). *Forms of talk.* Blackwell: Oxford.

Gottman, J. M., & Markman, H. J. (1978). Experimental designs in psychotherapy research. In S. L. Garfield & A. E. Bergin (Eds.), *Handbook of psychotherapy and behavior change: An empirical analysis* (pp. 23–62). New York: John Wiley & Sons.

Greenberg, L. S. (1982). Psychotherapy process research. In E. Walker (Ed.), *Handbook of clinical psychotherapy* (pp. 164–204). New York: Dorsey.

Greenberg, L. S. (1984). Task analysis: The general approach. In L. N. Rice & L. S. Greenberg (Eds.), *Patterns of change: Intensive analysis of psychotherapy process* (pp. 124–148). New York: The Guilford Press.

Greenberg, L. S. (1986a). Change process research. *Journal of Consulting and Clinical Psychology, 54*(1), 4–9.

Greenberg, L. S. (1986b). Research strategies. In L. S. Greenberg & W. M. Pinsof (Eds.), *The psychotherapeutic process: A research handbook.* New York: The Guilford Press.

Greenberg, L. S. (1989). Book review of L. C. Wynne (Ed.), *State of the art in family therapy research. Journal of Marital and Family Therapy, 15*(2), 207–208.

Greenberg, L. S., & Pinsof, W. (1986). Process research: Current trends and future perspectives. In L. Greenberg & W. Pinsof (Eds.), *The psychotherapeutic process: A research handbook* (pp. 3–20). New York: Guilford.

Gurman, A. S. (1988). Issues in the specification of family therapy interventions. In L. C. Wynne (Ed.), *The state of the art in family therapy research: Controversies and recommendations* (pp. 125–138). New York: Family Process Press.

Gurman, A. S., & Kniskern, D. P. (1978). Research on marital and family therapy: Progress, perspective, and prospect. In S. L. Garfield & A. E. Bergin (Eds.),

Handbook of psychotherapy and behavior change: An empirical analysis (pp. 817–902). New York: John Wiley & Sons.

Gurman, A. S., & Kniskern, D. P. (1981). Family therapy outcome research: Knowns and unknowns. In A. S. Gurman & D. P. Kniskern (Eds.), *Handbook of family therapy* (pp. 742–776). New York: Brunner/Mazel, Inc.

Gurman, A. S., Kniskern, D. P., & Pinsof, W. M. (1986). Research on the process and outcome of marital and family therapy. In S. L. Garfield & A. E. Bergin (Eds.), *Handbook of psychotherapy and behavior change* (pp. 565–623). New York: John Wiley & Sons.

Haley, J., & Hoffman, L. (1967). *Techniques of family therapy.* New York: Basic Books.

Heritage, J. (1984). *Garfinkel and Ethnomethodology.* Cambridge, England: Polity Press.

Heritage, J. (1988). Explanations as accounts: A conversation analytic perspective. In C. Antaki's (Ed.), *Analysing everyday explanation: A casebook of methods* (pp. 127–144). London: Sage Publications.

Hoffman, L. (1981). *Foundations of family therapy.* New York: Basic Books.

Hopper, R. (1988). Speech, for instance. The exemplar in studies of conversation. *Journal of Language and Social Psychology, 7*(1), 47–63.

Hopper, R., & Koch, S. (1986). *How to do things with conversational analysis: A practical methods manual.* Unpublished manuscript.

Hoshmand, L. T. (1989). Alternate research paradigms: A review and teaching proposal. *The Counseling Psychologist, 17*(1), 3–79.

Jacobs, S., & Jackson, S. (1989, May). *Reliability and validity in discourse analysis.* Paper presented at the International Communication Association Conference, San Francisco, CA.

Keeney, B. P. (1982). What is an epistemology of family therapy? *Family Process, 21*(02), 153–168.

Keeney, B. P. (1983). *Aesthetics of change.* New York: Guilford Press.

Keeney, B. P. (1986). *The therapeutic voice of Olga Silverstein.* New York: Guilford Press.

Kerlinger, F. N. (1973). *Foundations of behavioral research* (2nd ed.). New York: Holt, Rinehart and Winston.

Kiesler, D. J. (1973). *The process of psychotherapy: Empirical foundations and systems of analysis.* Chicago: Aldine.

Kiesler, D. J. (1986). Forward. In L. S. Greenberg & W. M. Pinsof (Eds.), *The psychotherapeutic process: A research handbook* (pp. vii–xi). New York: The Guilford Press.

Lennard, H. L., & Bernstein, A. (1960). *The anatomy of psychotherapy: Systems of communication and expectation.* New York: Columbia University Press.

Levinson, S. (1983). *Pragmatics.* Cambridge: Cambridge University Press.

Luborsky, L. (1972). Research cannot yet influence clinical practice. In A. E. Bergin & H. H. Strupp (Eds.), *Changing frontiers in the science of psychotherapy* pp. 120–127). Chicago: Aldine Atherton.

Mahrer, A. R. (1985). *Psychotherapeutic change: An alternative approach to meaning and measurement.* New York: W. W. Norton & Company.

Mahrer, A. R. (1988). Discovery-oriented psychotherapy research. *American Psychologist, 43*(9), 694–702.

Mahrer A. R., Dessaulles, A., Nadler, W. P., Gervaize, P. A., & Sterner, I. (1987). Good and very good moments in psychotherapy: Content, distribution, and facilitation. *Psychotherapy, 24*(1), 7–14.

Mahrer, A. R., & Nadler, W. P. (1986). Good moments in psychotherapy: A preliminary review, a list, and some promising research avenues. *Journal of Consulting and Clinical Psychology, 54*(1), 10–15.

O'Hanlon, B., & Wilk, J. (1987). *Shifting contexts: The generation of effective psychotherapy.* New York: Guilford Press.

O'Hanlon, W. H. (1987). *Taproots: Underlying principles of Milton Erickson's therapy and hypnosis.* New York: W. W. Norton & Company.

O'Hanlon, W. H. (1989). *A grand unified theory for brief therapy: Putting problems in context.* Unpublished manuscript.

O'Hanlon, W. H., & Weiner-Davis, M. (1989). *In search of solutions: A new direction in psychotherapy.* New York: W. W. Norton & Company.

Orlinsky, D. E., & Howard, K. I. (1978). The relation of process to outcome in psychotherapy. In S. L. Garfield & A. E. Bergin (Eds.), *Handbook of psychotherapy and behavior change: An empirical analysis* (2nd ed., pp. 283–330). New York: John Wiley & Sons.

Parloff, M. B., Waskow, I. E., & Wolfe, B. E. (1978). Research on therapist variables in relation to process and outcome. In S. L. Garfield & A. E. Bergin (Eds.), *Handbook of psychotherapy and behavior change: An empirical analysis* (pp. 233–282). New York: John Wiley & Sons.

Pearce, W. B., & Cronen, V. E. (1980). *Communication, action, and meaning: The creation of the social realities.* New York: Praeger Publishers.

Pinsof, W. M. (1981). Family therapy process research. In A.S. Gurman & D. P. Kniskern (Eds.), *Handbook of family therapy* (pp. 699–741). New York: Brunner/Mazel.

Pinsof, W. M. (1986). The process of family therapy: The development of the family therapist coding system. In L. S. Greenberg & W. M. Pinsof (Eds.), *The psychotherapeutic process: A research handbook* (pp. 201–284). New York: The Guilford Press.

Pinsof, W. M. (1988). Strategies for the study of family therapy research. In L. C. Wynne (Ed.), *The state of the art in family therapy research: Controversies and recommendations* (pp. 159–174). New York: Family Process Press.

Pomerantz, A. (1987). Pursuing a response. In J. M. Atkinson & J. Heritage (Eds.), *Structure of social action: Studies in conversation analysis* (pp. 152–164). Cambridge: Cambridge University Press.

Pomerantz, A. (1988). Offering a candidate answer: An information-seeking strategy. *Communication Monographs, 55,* 360–373.

Pomerantz, A., & Atkinson, J. M. (1984). Ethnomethodology, conversation analysis and the study of courtroom interaction. In D. J. Muller, D. E. Blackman, & A. J. Chapman (Eds.), *Topics in Psychology and Law* (pp. 283–297). Chichester: Wiley.

Potter, J., & Wetherell, M. (1987). *Discourse and social psychology: Beyond attitudes and behavior.* London: Sage Publications.

Rawot, D. J. (1989). Challenging the status quo: Epistemology and Erickson. *Family Therapy News, 20*(2), 10.

Reiss, D. (1988). Theoretical versus tactical inferences: Or how to do family therapy research without dying of boredom. In L. C. Wynne (Ed.), *The state of the art in family therapy research: Controversies and recommendations* (pp. 33–46). New York: Family Process Press.

Rice, L. N., & Greenberg, L. S. (Eds.). (1984a). *Patterns of change: Intensive analysis of psychotherapy process.* New York: The Guilford Press.

Rice, L. N., & Greenberg, L. S. (1984b). The new research paradigm. In L. N. Rice & L. S. Greenberg (Eds.), *Patterns of change: Intensive analysis of psychotherapy process* (pp. 7–26). New York: The Guilford Press.

Rice, L. N., & Kerr, G. P. (1986). Measures of client and therapist vocal quality. In L. S. Greenberg & W. M. Pinsof (Eds.), *The psychotherapeutic process: A research handbook.* New York: The Guilford Press.

Rogers, C. R. (1942). The use of electrically recorded interviews in improving psychotherapeutic techniques. *American Journal of Orthopsychiatry, 12,* 429–434.

Russell, R. L. (1987). Introduction. In R. L. Russell (Ed.), *Language in psychotherapy: Strategies of discovery* (pp. 1–12). New York: Plenum Press.

Sacks, H. (1987). Notes on methodology. In J. M. Atkinson & J. Heritage (Eds.), *Structures of social action: Studies in conversation analysis* (pp. 21–27). Cambridge: Cambridge University Press.

Sacks, H., Schegloff, E. A., & Jefferson, G. (1974). A simplist systematics for the organization of turn-taking for conversation. *Language, 50,* 696–735.

Safran, J. D., Greenberg, L. S., & Rice, L. N. (1988). Integrating psychotherapy research and practice: Modeling the change process. *Psychotherapy, 25(1),* 1–17.

Scheflen, A. E. (1973). *Communicational structure: Analysis of a psychotherapy transaction.* Bloomington: Indiana University Press.

Schegloff, E. A., & Sacks, H. (1973). Opening up closings. *Semiotica, 7,* 289–327.

Schenkein, J. N. (1978). *Studies in the organization of conversational interaction.* New York: Academic Press.

Schwartz, H., & Jacobs, J. (1979). *Qualitative sociology: A method to the madness.* London: The Free Press.

Schwartzman, J. (1984). Family theory and the scientific method. *Family Process, 23,* 223–236.

Segal, L., & Bavelas, J. B. (1983). Human systems and communication theory. In B. B. Wolman & G. Sticker (Eds.), *Handbook of family and marital therapy.* New York: Plenum.

Sigman, J. S., Sullivan, S. J., & Wendell, M. (1986). Conversational structure. In C. H. Tardy (Ed.), *Instrumentation in communication* (pp. 163–192). Norwood, NJ: Ablex.

Small, J. J., & Manthei R. J. (1986). The language of therapy. *Psychotherapy, 23(3),* 395–404.

Stanton, M. D. (1988). The lobster quadrille: Issues and dilemmas for family therapy research. In L. C. Wynne (Ed.), *The state of the art in family therapy research: Controversies and recommendations* (pp. 5–32). New York: Family Process Press.

Steier, F. (1985). Toward a cybernetic methodology of family therapy research: Fitting research methods to family practice. In L. L. Andreozzi (Ed.), *Integra-*

ting research and clinical practice (pp. 27–36). Rockville, MD: Aspen Publication.

Steier, F. (1988). Toward a coherent methodology for the study of family therapy. In L. C. Wynne (Ed.), *The state of the art in family therapy research: Controversies and recommendations* (pp. 227–234). New York: Family Process Press.

Strupp, H. H. (1973). *Psychotherapy: Clinical, research, and theoretical issues.* New York: Jason Aronson, Inc.

Szasz, T. (1978). *The myth of psychotherapy.* New York: Anchor Books.

Tomm, K. (1983). The old hat doesn't fit. *Family Therapy Networker, 7,* 39–41.

Tyler, S. A. (1978). *The said and the unsaid: Mind, meaning, and culture.* New York: Academic Press.

Varela, F. J. (1989). Reflections on the circulation of concepts between a biology of cognition and systemic family therapy. *Family Process, 28*(1), 15–24.

Watzlawick, P., Bavelas, J. B., & Jackson, D. D. (1967). *The pragmatics of human communication.* New York: W. W. Norton & Company.

Weakland, J. H. (1987). Forword. In B. O'Hanlon & J. Wilk's *Shifting Contexts: The generation of effective psychotherapy* (pp. vii–viii). New York: The Guilford Press.

Wynne, L. C. (1985). Foreword. In S. de Shazer's *Keys to solution in brief therapy* (pp. vii–ix). New York: W. W. Norton & Company.

Wynne, L. C. (Ed.). (1988a). *The state of the art in family therapy research: Controversies and recommendations.* New York: Family Process Press.

Wynne, L. C. (1988b). The presenting problem and theory based family variables: Keystones for family therapy research. In L. C. Wynne (Ed.), *The state of the art in family therapy research: Controversies and recommendations* (pp. 89–108). New York: Family Process Press.

Wynne, L. C. (1988c). An overview of the state of the art: What should be expected in current family therapy research. In L. C. Wynne (Ed.), *The state of the art in family therapy research: Controversies and recommendations* (pp. 249–266). New York: Family Process Press.

Author Index

Subject Index